Teaching the NAEYC Code of Ethical Conduct: A Resource Guide

Teaching the NAEYC Code of Ethical Conduct: A Resource Guide

Stephanie Feeney, Nancy K. Freeman, and Eva Moravcik

Companion Resource to *Ethics and the Early Childhood Educator: Using the NAEYC Code, Second Edition*

National Association for the Education of Young Children

naeyc®

National Association for the
Education of Young Children

National Association for the Education
of Young Children
1313 L Street NW, Suite 500
Washington, DC 20005-4101
202-232-8777 • 800-424-2460
www.naeyc.org

NAEYC Books

Senior Director, Content Strategy
and Development
Susan Friedman

Editor-in-Chief
Kathy Charner

Senior Creative Design Manager
Audra Meckstroth

Managing Editor
Mary Jaffe

Senior Editor
Holly Bohart

Senior Graphic Designer
Malini Dominey

Associate Editor
Heather Benson Collick

Editorial Assistant
Ryan Smith

Through its publications program, the
National Association for the Education
of Young Children (NAEYC) provides
a forum for discussion of major issues
and ideas in the early childhood field.
We hope to provoke thought and
promote professional growth. The
views expressed or implied in this
book are not necessarily those of the
Association.

Activities in the Appendix are intended for use
in group settings and may be reproduced for
educational and training purposes only.

Library of Congress Control Number:
2016936331

ISBN: 978-1-938113-22-2

NAEYC Item #1181

Contents

Preface

Over the years we have been involved with NAEYC's work on professional ethics, we have come to believe that the moral commitment to children and their families should be at the heart of our work. We believe that all early childhood educators should be aware of their moral responsibilities, should know the NAEYC Code of Ethical Conduct, and should develop skill applying it to real-life situations. We have written this book to promote greater awareness, understanding, and use of the Code.

This book is intended for you if you are a trainer, a program administrator who provides staff development, or a teacher in a two- or four-year teacher preparation program. You are probably consulting this book because you are planning to teach a one-time ethics workshop, a conference session, or a class meeting. Or you might be preparing to lead a series of workshops, several class sessions, or a whole course addressing early childhood educators' responsibilities to children and families. As an adult educator, you are no doubt aware that early childhood educators have moral obligations to the adults and children with whom they work and to the communities they serve, and you know that those who work with young children are likely to encounter many ethical issues in their work. You also know that it is worthwhile for those who work with young children to be familiar with and use the Code of Ethical Conduct of their professional association—NAEYC.

The previous edition of this book, *Teaching the NAEYC Code of Ethical Conduct: Activity Sourcebook,* was published in 2000 (updated 2008) as a companion to the first edition of *Ethics and the Early Childhood Educator* (Feeney & Freeman 1999). It was written to assist those who teach early childhood educators about professional ethics and the NAEYC Code. This new edition has been revised to align with the second edition of *Ethics and the Early Childhood Educator* (Feeney, Freeman, & Pizzolongo 2012) and the most recent (2005/2011) revision of the NAEYC Code of Ethical Conduct.

The first edition of this book focused primarily on activities that could be used to teach about professional ethics. The name of this edition has changed to *Teaching the NAEYC Code of Ethical Conduct: A Resource Guide* to indicate that the focus has expanded. This new edition includes a stronger rationale for the teaching of ethics and more guidance for planning learning experiences to meet the needs of individuals who work in a variety of settings and who have varying levels of professional experience. It still contains many activities designed to help learners acquire essential information about morality, ethics, and the NAEYC Code of Ethics. Some of these activities have been updated and a number of new ones have been added.

This new edition is intended to help you to understand the

- Moral aspects of work with young children
- Role of ethics in a profession

- Needs of adult learners at different stages of professional development
- Theories of moral development and their implications for ethical decision making
- Ways of teaching about the NAEYC Code of Ethical Conduct that are consistent with the Core Values that underlie the Code itself
- Ways of supporting the development of ethical reasoning

This book is organized into seven chapters. The first two provide a context for teaching about professional ethics. The next four offer suggestions for curriculum planning and activities. The seventh and final chapter deals with assessment of students' learning and of your teaching.

Chapter 1—Teaching Professional Ethics addresses instructional formats, how instruction can be tailored for learners with different levels of experience, how to sequence ethics instruction, determining the goals of ethics instruction, and selecting strategies for getting started in your teaching.

Chapter 2—Know the Learner discusses stages of professional development and stages of moral development in adult learners. It explores how this knowledge can inform curriculum design and teaching of professional ethics.

Chapter 3—Teaching About Morality and Ethics explores how to teach about personal and professional morality and professional values and ethics.

Chapter 4—Teaching the NAEYC Code of Ethical Conduct presents information about how to teach the content and application of NAEYC's Code.

Chapter 5—Addressing Ethical Issues focuses on how to teach learners to distinguish between ethical responsibilities and ethical dilemmas, strategies for helping students learn to resolve ethical dilemmas, and how you can support the development of higher levels of ethical reasoning.

Chapter 6—Putting the Pieces Together contains examples of how the authors have designed ethics trainings for a variety of audiences in a number of different settings.

Chapter 7— Assessing Learning and Evaluating Teaching Effectiveness provides suggestions for how you can acquire information about student learning and about the effectiveness of your teaching.

The **Appendix** contains directions for activities, games, and materials that you can reproduce to use in your teaching.

It is important to remember that this book does not stand alone—it is a companion designed to help you to effectively teach the contents of *Ethics and the Early Childhood Educator* (Feeney, Freeman, & Pizzolongo 2012).

The professional preparation that most early childhood adult educators receive is in child development and early childhood education. Few of us have had an ethics course, and fewer still have had training in how to teach professional ethics. This book is an attempt to fill this gap. We hope that the information provided here will help you to design effective ethics instruction and demonstrate to the early childhood educators with whom you work that there is a strong connection between the Core Values, Ideals, and Principles in the NAEYC Code of Ethical Conduct and the moral nature of their day-to-day work with children and families.

—Stephanie Feeney, Nancy K. Freeman, and Eva Moravcik

One

Teaching Professional Ethics

This introductory chapter is designed to provide a context for the teaching of **professional ethics** in early childhood education. In it we discuss different instructional formats, show how instruction can be tailored for learners with different levels of experience, suggest an approach to sequencing instruction, look at setting goals and ways you can prepare yourself to teach **ethics**, and offer some strategies for getting started. How instruction is organized will of course depend on the purpose and context of the training, how much experience the learners have had with young children (their level of maturity and stage of **moral development**), and their previous exposure to professional ethics.

Instructional Formats

Ethics trainings can range from informal experiences, like a discussion in a child care center, to formal ones, such as college courses taken for credit. They can occur in a variety of settings, be of different durations, and have different goals. As an adult educator you plan very differently for veteran teachers in an in-service workshop than you do for a group of undergraduate students in an introductory course, or for a session at a conference that may be participants' first exposure to ethics in early childhood education.

Ethics. The study of right and wrong, or duty and obligation, that involves critical reflection on morality and the ability to make choices between values and the examination of the moral dimensions of relationships.

Moral development. The emergence and change in moral understanding from infancy through adulthood. Increasing ability over time to distinguish right from wrong.

Professional ethics. The moral commitments of a profession that involve moral reflection that extends and enhances the personal morality practitioners bring to their work, that concern actions of right and wrong in the workplace, and that help individuals resolve moral dilemmas they encounter in their work.

Values. Qualities or principles that individuals believe to be desirable or worthwhile and that they prize for themselves, for others, and for the world in which they live.

In-Service Education

In-service education in professional ethics can be conducted by a director who is helping staff members learn about a **code of ethics** or address some of the thorny **ethical issues** they encounter in their work. It can be conducted by an experienced early childhood educator who is offering a local, state, or national conference presentation for teachers or directors, or it can be offered by a professional development specialist who provides community training (e.g., for a Head Start program or a state's QRIS—Quality Rating and Improvement System).

Code of ethics. Defines the core values of the field and provides guidance for what professionals should do when they encounter conflicting obligations or responsibilities in their work.

Core values. Commitments held by a profession that are consciously and knowingly embraced by its practitioners because they make a contribution to society. There is a difference between personal values and the core values of a profession.

Ethical issues. Situations that involve determining what is right and wrong, and what rights and responsibilities and issues of human welfare are part of the situation.

Your goal for either a one-time training or ongoing in-service professional development is to improve participants' day-to-day practice. Tailoring instruction to the learners is not difficult if you are working with a group of teachers you know and who are dealing with real-life ethical situations. When there is a shared commitment to the profession's **core values**, regularly scheduled staff meetings that include open-ended explorations of ethical issues can be especially fruitful.

When working with teachers you do not know, such as at a workshop or conference, your task is to make the learning experiences meaningful and applicable to practitioners with varying levels of professional preparation and experience. This book is designed to help you to do that.

College Courses

All accredited teacher preparation institutions offering initial and advanced degrees in early childhood education are now required to include professional ethics in their core curriculum. Sometimes professional ethics is included in an introductory (foundations) course or a course on professionalism; in other instances it is a strand in several courses such as child development and working with families, and then revisited in practicum courses, student teaching seminars, and program culmination (capstone) courses. Some institutions combine these approaches.

The important point is that instruction in ethics must be explicit and must be included in course syllabi. If it is not a formalized part of the curriculum, everyone might assume that someone else is teaching it and, in the end, ethics might not be adequately addressed during students' professional preparation.

If you are teaching ethics in a college course you probably have a good idea what the students are like and you may know some of them. In this setting you will be responsible for planning the content and also for assessing students' learning.

Tailoring Instruction for Different Levels of Experience

Following are some broad guidelines for designing instruction for learners who are at different stages in their professional development and learning.

Working With Beginners

Create learning experiences for beginners that include content that is practical and engaging and that

- Requires little experience or initiative
- Provides basic information
- Connects to and draws upon the learners' life experiences
- Makes ethics real
- Promotes active participation

Working With Experienced Educators

Learning experiences for experienced early childhood educators can provide opportunities for them to

- Share their professional experiences
- Apply their previous professional experiences
- Acquire advanced information
- Develop skill in applying the NAEYC Code
- Develop skill in reasoning and **ethical deliberation**
- Develop skill in justifying ethical decisions

Working With Both Beginning and Experienced Educators

A class, workshop, or staff training may include both beginning and experienced educators with varying degrees of knowledge and experience. Such diversity provides differences in perspective that can be challenging but may also prove valuable as you help individuals expand their understanding of professional ethics.

How to Identify Activities for Different Learners

Chapters 1, 3, 4, and 5 have activities that are designed to help students get to know each other and learn about and apply the NAEYC Code of Ethical Conduct. Each activity is identified as Icebreaker (Introductory), Beginning, Intermediate, or Advanced. The Icebreaker activities in this chapter are designed to help participants get to know each other. Beginning activities are designed to promote understanding of basic concepts related to ethics and introduce the Code. Intermediate activities expand on basic knowledge of the Code. Advanced activities involve application and are for those who are acquainted with the Code and familiar with the process of ethical analysis.

Ethical deliberation. Careful thought or discussion of ethical issues in order to make a decision.

With mixed groups, it is helpful to

- Begin with an orientation to make sure everyone has some basic understanding of the ethical dimensions of working with young children
- Include real-life examples to make the topic come alive for everyone
- Allow time and opportunities for participants to share their experiences with others
- Acknowledge what each participant contributes

The Sequence of Ethics Instruction

Ethics instruction logically progresses from creating an awareness of ethical issues in early childhood education and the existence of a code of ethics to developing participants' skills in applying the code and engaging in **moral reasoning**.

In their article "A Developmental Approach to Teaching About Ethics Using the NAEYC Code of Ethical Conduct," Holly Brophy-Herb, Marjorie Kostelnik, and Laura Stein (2001) describe a four-phase developmental model of educators' increasing understanding of ethics. It provides a useful outline for the design of ethics instruction.

1. *Awareness.* Individuals focus on the personal **values** that govern their lives, the values represented in their professional code, and the specific substance of that code.

2. *Differentiating **ethical judgments** from other judgments.* Emphasizes helping individuals make distinctions between ethical judgments and other kinds of judgments.

3. *Analyzing **ethical dilemmas**.* Individuals apply a systematic approach to resolving ethical dilemmas.

4. *Applying the NAEYC Code in daily practice.* Individuals learn how to translate ethical thinking into ethical conduct.

Ethical dilemma. A moral conflict that involves determining appropriate conduct when an individual faces conflicting professional values and responsibilities. (A dilemma has two defensible resolutions.)

Ethical judgment. (Terms with a similar meaning are moral judgment, ethical decision making, and ethical analysis.) The ability to make moral distinctions, understand moral concepts, and engage in increasingly higher levels of **moral reasoning**.

Moral reasoning. The ability to understand moral concepts and to engage in increasingly higher levels of moral reflection; deliberation by which an individual determines alternatives that are morally right and morally wrong.

We recommend a sequence of training that is consistent with this framework. First, help learners acquire an awareness of their personal values, introduce them to the NAEYC Code of Ethical Conduct, and help them see how it is relevant to their work. Next, help them understand how ethical issues are different from other kinds of issues they will encounter in their work with young children. Then help them to develop skills to systematically address issues using the NAEYC Code and learn to clearly explain their ethical positions. The final component is to promote learners' readiness and ability to use the Code in their daily practice as a decision-making tool.

Determine Your Objectives

It is crucial to clarify what you want to accomplish—your objectives. In part, you base your objectives on the kind of education you are offering and the kind of learners with whom you are working.

Some appropriate objectives for ethics instruction include helping learners

- Become aware of the personal values and **morality** that they bring to the workplace
- Become aware that moral commitments are an essential part of a profession and have special importance for early childhood educators
- Understand the difference between personal values and morality, and professional ethics
- Become familiar with the NAEYC Code of Ethical Conduct that can help them address the ethical issues that occur in work with young children and their families
- Differentiate ethical issues from other kinds of issues
- Understand the difference between **professional responsibilities** and ethical dilemmas
- Understand the kinds of ethical dilemmas that occur in early childhood settings and how to identify the stakeholders involved
- Learn to use the NAEYC Code of Ethical Conduct to process an ethical dilemma
- Learn to use guidance from the Code in combination with professional judgment to reach an informed and defensible resolution to an ethical dilemma
- Increase **ethical commitment**—apply what they have learned about ethics and ethical analysis in their workplace

Ethical commitment. Intention to apply learning about ethical responsibilities and ethical analysis in the workplace.

Morality. People's views of what is good, right, and proper; their beliefs about their obligations; and their ideas about how they should behave.

Professional responsibilities. (Also referred to as ethical responsibilities.) Behaviors that one must or must not engage in. Ethical responsibilities are clear-cut and are spelled out in the Code of Ethical Conduct.

You will choose one or two appropriate objectives for a one-time workshop, or several for a course or series of workshops. The objectives you select and how you describe them will depend on how accountable you are for students' learning. In a short workshop your goal is likely to develop awareness. If you are teaching a workshop for professional development credit or a college course, you may write specific objectives and use appropriate assessments to determine if your objectives have been achieved.

Plan Instruction

Once you are clear on your objectives and have thought about the characteristics and needs of the learners, you can begin to plan your teaching. Consider how much time is available for your workshop or class session. Most in-service training is conducted in fairly brief sessions (generally between one and two hours). In a one-time workshop or a single class session, you can build awareness and provide some basic information. A series of sessions or classes over a period of weeks or months provides more opportunities for participants to read, reflect, and apply what they are learning.

Chapters 3, 4, and 5 contain suggestions for teaching each of the topics included in *Ethics and the Early Childhood Educator*. Chapter 6 gives some examples of how training sessions and courses can be structured to help students gain awareness, knowledge, and skills related to ethics.

Prepare Yourself

There are two important aspects of preparing yourself to teach ethics. The first is to reflect on your own experience with ethics and your knowledge and commitment to furthering awareness and understanding of ethical behavior in early childhood education. The second is to have a strong grounding in what you are about to teach. Carefully read the Code and the applicable sections of *Ethics and the Early Childhood Educator*. If you are doing training that is in-depth or more advanced than a basic introduction, you should be familiar with the major theories of moral development and the fundamentals of ethical theory, as well as the characteristics of practitioners at various stages in their professional lives (discussed in Chapter 2, beginning on page 11). You should also be familiar with any other codes of ethical conduct that apply to those with whom you are working.

As you begin to plan, decide which resources you want to use. If you are conducting a brief introductory workshop, you simply may call the group's attention to the book *Ethics and the Early Childhood Educator* and then make sure that each person has a copy of the most recent version of the *NAEYC Code of Ethical Conduct and Statement of Commitment* (NAEYC 2005/2011). If you are teaching ethics as part of a course or conducting a training series on ethics, it will be helpful to assign or make available copies of the book for all of the participants.

Regardless of the experience level of the group or the format of the training, we suggest that you

- Begin with activities that build awareness (some introductory activities are included at the end of this chapter)
- Provide opportunities for participants to reflect on their personal experiences (the reflection questions in each chapter of *Ethics and the Early Childhood Educator* are designed for that purpose)

- Choose activities that balance opportunities for taking in information in the form of reading or listening to a lecture with opportunities for expressing ideas and integrating new learning through active involvement in discussions and games
- Allow time for participants to share personal experiences and concerns

In a credit-bearing workshop or college class, you can help learners feel more prepared by assigning reading materials or a reflection assignment prior to meeting for the first time.

Getting Started

Adults, like children, need transitions that help them shift their focus and prepare for learning. If the learners do not know each other, you will need to establish a sense of comfort. A group of students or colleagues who know each other well may need some time to greet one another before they can bring their attention to the topic of the session. In either case it is a good idea to plan time for an introductory activity that meets this need for your group.

Adult learners like to know the purpose of training sessions and what they can expect so that they are confident that their time will be well spent. It is a good idea to share a statement of purpose (verbally, or on a chart or PowerPoint presentation) and identify the intended learning outcomes at the beginning of the session. Posting an agenda to give participants information about the sequence of the training is also helpful.

Build a sense of trust. Effective lessons on ethics often begin with a warm-up or icebreaking activity designed to lay the groundwork for developing trust. The last section of this chapter includes a number of activities that may be helpful for introducing a training or class session.

Because the discussion of ethics involves sharing personal feelings and experiences, it is important to build a sense of community among members of the group. This is particularly important when participants are engaged in discussions of values, morality, ethics, and appropriate and inappropriate professional behavior. Warm-up activities can contribute to the creation of a nonthreatening atmosphere in which participants feel comfortable enough to share freely without fear of criticism or judgment.

Since discussions of ethical issues may bring to light differing values and beliefs, and often involve sharing personal experiences, it is especially important to establish ground rules that will create a nonthreatening environment where participants can trust that their views will be respected and confidences honored. Clearly laying out these rules for the group at the outset helps prevent problems and is a good way to build a sense of trust.

If your discussions are likely to include sensitive real-life situations, it is essential that you address the issue of confidentiality. It is also important to be aware of individuals' reactions. Steer participants away from judgmental behavior and statements.

We often post ground rules at the beginning of a session and ask the group to agree to them, add to them, or revise them. Here are some basic ground rules we have used in ethics sessions:

- Participate—there are many ways of participating, including listening to others
- Honor other people's opinions and questions—no one will be put down or disregarded because of his or her opinions or questions
- Maintain confidentiality—what is shared here will remain within this group and will not be discussed elsewhere
- Pause after someone's comments to allow the group time to reflect on them

When we are teaching a college class, we add another rule:

- Handle problems responsibly with the person with whom you have the problem—don't complain to others or gossip. (We volunteer to serve as mediator if this is necessary.)

Lay a foundation. After the warm-up activities we begin every training session with a review of foundational material, including definitions and an overview of the NAEYC Code of Ethical Conduct, so that everyone involved in a discussion has the same information. When we have done sessions without doing this kind of introduction, we have invariably found that people understood important terms in very different ways. (You can find a detailed description of these terms in Chapter 1, "An Introduction to Morality and Ethics," in *Ethics and the Early Childhood Educator*.) We also discuss the role of ethics in professions and the need for early childhood educators to have strong moral commitments to children and families.

The strategies and activities presented in the chapters that follow provide many ideas about how to present ethics content in in-service training and class sessions.

Introductory Activities

Introductory activities are designed to help participants get to know and become comfortable with one another. They are not specifically related to ethics. If you have time, one or more of these activities can help to break the ice in a class or workshop. If time is limited (e.g., a one-time 1–2 hour workshop), you might just have students introduce themselves and share one thing that might be of interest to the group.

Activity 1.1: Match-Ups (Icebreaker)

This activity presents a list of questions about the learner's childhood ("How old were you when you first went to school?" or "What was your favorite place to play?"). Give everyone a list of questions (the list for Activity 1.1 is on page 95 of the Appendix). Participants fill in their answers, then they try to find someone whose answer matches theirs.

Activity 1.2: Scavenger Hunt (Icebreaker)

This activity presents a list of statements (unrelated to ethics) that are likely to describe one or more of the participants ("Loves dogs" or "Teaches 3-year-olds") (statements for Activity 1.2 are on page 96 in the Appendix). Give each participant a copy of the list and then have them interview each other to find someone who matches each of the descriptors. When they find a match, they ask that person to initial the item on their sheet. To encourage participants to talk to one another, ask them to gather an interesting or unexpected related fact for each item (e.g., if someone says that he or she has lived in another country, ask that person where).

If the participants are a group of people who know each other well, you might interview them in advance to learn unexpected things others might not know and then use these as descriptors (e.g., "Took a college course on the Beatles," "Knows sign language").

Activity 1.3: BINGO (Icebreaker)

This introductory activity involves playing BINGO with a card that has descriptors similar to those in the Scavenger Hunt. (A reproducible BINGO card for Activity 1.3 is on page 97 of the Appendix.) Give everyone a card with a list of descriptors, making sure to have some that are unusual and many that are likely to be found in any group of early childhood educators. In this activity, speed is of the essence. Ask participants to walk around the room and talk to others. Have them ask each person they talk to initial the squares that apply to them. The first person to get a row filled with initials shouts "Bingo!" Then have a show of hands for each of the descriptors (all the cat owners raise their hands). You may wish to give a prize (e.g., a bookmark with the statement of commitment printed on it) to the winners.

Activity 1.4: Corners (Icebreaker)

This activity requires a room that is relatively free of furniture so that participants are able to move from corner to corner. Label the four corners of the room with signs (1-2-3-4, or north-south-east-west, or red-yellow-blue-green).

Describe a physical characteristic (e.g., brown hair) and ask participants with that characteristic to walk to corner 1. Send those with other hair colors to a different corner (black hair to corner 2, blond to corner 3, other colors to corner 4). Once everyone is in a corner, invite them to exchange greetings and start a conversation.

After a brief time repeat the activity, dividing the group in different ways—by statistics (born in this state, south/north, east/west of here), personal preferences (broccoli, carrots, pumpkin, or kale lovers), or experiences (horse, subway, bike, or motorcycle riders), or other personal categories similar to those in Activities 1.2 and 1.3 above. After allowing for several interchanges, call the groups together to begin your session.

Activities and Reflections

The chapters in this book include activities that you can use to actively engage participants in learning about professional ethics and the NAEYC Code. You can also assign the reflections included in *Ethics and the Early Childhood Educator* as a topic for journal entries or as preparation for your sessions, or use them as individual or small group class activities. Whether you use them as class preparation or during instructional time, reflections offer valuable opportunities for students to thoughtfully engage with ethical issues and discuss them with others.

As you plan your teaching, please keep in mind that the strategies and activities we present in this book are only suggestions. Adapt them according to the needs and characteristics of your setting and the group with whom you work.

Two

Know the Learner

Providing learning experiences that match the needs and interests of the learners is as important when teaching adults as it is when working with young children. Similarly, learning experiences that are appropriate for teaching ethics should vary based on the adult learners' characteristics, needs, and interests. When teaching a group about ethics, it is important to design instruction that addresses the needs of the group you are teaching as well as the needs of individual learners within the group, presenting ethics in ways that are flexible and responsive to individuals' and group interests, needs, questions, and concerns.

Before you start to plan a training session or course, consider the following questions about the learners:

- Are they likely to be beginning or experienced early childhood educators?
- What types of educational backgrounds will they have had?
- What kinds of work experiences are they likely to have had?
- How well do you think they will be able to engage in abstract thinking?

Remember, the long-term goal of understanding ethics is for early childhood educators to grow in their ability to engage in well-reasoned ethical deliberation. Once you have considered the answers to the questions posed above, think about what the particular learners with whom you are working need to know about ethics, and adjust your approach to address the specific objectives you wish to achieve.

This chapter explores how early childhood educators' developmental stage affects the way you teach professional ethics. It considers learners' developmental stages from two perspectives—professional development and moral development.

Stages of Professional Development

Lilian Katz (1995) has identified four developmental stages of early childhood educators. She describes the interests and needs of beginning teachers and explains how those

Throughout this book, the terms *learner, student, teacher,* or *participant* are used interchangeably and apply to those in credit-granting settings as well as those engaged in not-for-credit professional development.

interests and needs change as beginners grow into mature professionals. Figure 2.1, ***Stages of Professional Development,*** describes five career stages and the implications of teaching adults in each of them. It is based on Katz's model, but we have added an additional stage (novice) to refer to students who are preparing to work in the field of early childhood education. You can use these stages to plan professional experiences that are appropriate for the learners you are working with.

Figure 2.1: Stages of Professional Development

Stage	Characteristics	Concerns	Implications for Teaching
I: Novice	Preservice teachers preparing to work in early childhood programs.	Will I be able to work successfully with young children? Is the field of early childhood education for me?	For most students everything is new. Content needs to be engaging, and they need to see how what they learn will be useful to them in the future.
II: Survival	First or second year of working with young children. Teachers are learning to apply what they learned during their preservice coursework. Teaching may be stressful because everything is new, and because they may have unrealistically high expectations of themselves.	Surviving on the job and being accepted by colleagues.	Content should be relevant and applicable to classroom practice.

Stage	Characteristics	Concerns	Implications for Teaching
III: Consolidation	Second or third year of teaching. Teachers begin to consolidate their knowledge to create their personal approach to working with children and families.	Working successfully with individual children, solving problems.	Practical advice that they can apply to their particular situations. On-site coaching and technical assistance are particularly effective professional development strategies.
IV: Renewal	Third to fifth year of teaching. Teachers seek new knowledge, and have a greater sense of their professionalism. May enjoy attending conferences and workshops and be ready for theoretical as well as practical professional readings. May seek involvement in professional associations.	Maintaining their enthusiasm, learning about new developments in the field.	Application of new knowledge and principles to guide their work with children.
V: Maturity	Five or more years of working with young children. These teachers are secure in their professional identity and are likely to be interested in considering the values, issues, theories, and philosophies that underlie their work with young children.	How can I contribute to the field?	Reflecting on their personal experience, reading, studying, and mentoring others. Are ready for more theoretical professional reading.

Based on Katz (1995).

Application of Professional Development Stages to Ethics Instruction

Whether you work with preservice college students, beginning teachers with little specialized training, or well-educated, experienced teachers, your first task is ensuring that they have a foundation in professional ethics that includes knowledge of the moral aspects of early childhood education, the NAEYC Code of Ethical Conduct, the difference between ethical responsibilities and ethical dilemmas, and how to use the Code to come to defensible resolutions for ethical dilemmas.

Working with beginners (college students and teachers at the survival stage). The ethical aspects of an early childhood educator's work often may not seem very real or important to college students and beginning teachers who are trying to gain mastery of teaching skills, such as planning learning experiences, leading a group time, and addressing children's challenging behaviors.

Preservice early childhood education students and beginning teachers often have questions that are immediate and concrete:

- How do I get the children to pay attention to what I say?
- How should I handle a disruptive child?
- What should I do tomorrow?
- How do I create a functional classroom?
- How can I organize my work so that I get everything done?
- How can I work effectively with families?
- How can I find out what children have learned and communicate it to their families and to program administrators?

College students and beginning teachers can learn important things about morality and ethics if you make what you teach practical and relevant to their day-to-day work with children and families. The most important thing to teach at this stage is that there is a Code, and that it is a valuable resource that will help them understand their moral responsibilities and address the ethical issues they face in the classroom.

A beginning teacher is likely to first encounter professional ethics in an introductory course or in a preservice training program. Even though beginners are likely to be focused on practical teaching skills, they benefit from learning about the ethical dimensions of teaching early in their careers. Instruction in professional ethics will help them focus on the field's shared values and commitments, making it clear that they are not just doing a job—they are joining a professional community (Sanger, Osguthorpe, & Fenstermacher 2013). They can learn to distinguish ethical issues from other kinds of issues and to identify the characteristics of professional responsibilities and ethical dilemmas. They can also benefit from being introduced to the framework for ethical decision making presented in *Ethics and the Early Childhood Educator*.

Beginners need information that they can use now, so they might not engage in sophisticated ethical deliberation. However, they may be enthusiastic about knowing and using the NAEYC Code when they see that it can help them address some of the difficult issues they encounter daily in their classrooms.

Working with mid-career teachers (consolidation and renewal stages). Experienced early childhood educators who have mastered basic teaching skills have more energy to focus on questions that have an ethical component, such as

- How do I talk with a mother who asks me to do something I don't think is good for her child?
- What should I do when I am not able to meet the needs of all of the children in my group?
- Should I say something if some of my colleagues are teaching in ways that I don't think are appropriate for young children?
- What can I do if the assessment instrument my director says I should use does not help me to improve instruction?
- How should I respond when a volunteer in my classroom asks me for personal information about a child or family?

The topic of ethics is likely to be very real to these more experienced teachers, although they may not know that ethics are involved in some of the issues they face. For these teachers, a greater understanding of the ethical dimensions of their work and help in learning to resolve ethical dilemmas may be very meaningful. It will not be difficult to involve them in workshop or course content on ethics. They are apt to bring many real-life experiences to discussions of the moral dimensions of teaching.

Teachers at this stage in their professional development are likely to know that there is a code of ethics for early childhood educators. They are ready for opportunities to delve more deeply into it, and may want guidance on how to systematically address ethical issues. They will benefit from opportunities to use the Code to identify ethical responsibilities, to seek resolutions to real-life ethical dilemmas, and to explain the rationale for the ethical decisions that they make.

Working with veterans (maturity stage). Teachers who have had many years of experience and who have acquired some professional wisdom are likely to appreciate that knowing about ethics is both an important professional responsibility and a valuable resource. Teachers in this stage of development may be able to identify the ethical responsibilities and ethical dilemmas they encounter in their workplace and to analyze ethical dilemmas in order to reach justifiable resolutions. They may be interested in learning about the role of ethics in professions and exploring the philosophic basis and moral principles that undergird the development of codes of ethics. Some emerging leaders in the field may also be eager for guidance about how they might share their knowledge of the Code in their workplace and other settings.

These practitioners are likely to be eager to share their experiences and will want to find good resolutions to issues they are confronting. Activities in an advanced course or workshop should allow them time to share their experiences as they develop a deeper understanding of the ethical dimensions of teaching and give them opportunities to hone their skills in the systematic analysis of ethical dilemmas.

The Deepening of Ethical Understanding Over Time

Teachers in the survival and consolidation stages of professional development are likely to consider ethical issues as presenting black-and-white choices, as having definite right or wrong answers. More experienced early childhood educators bring a nuanced and sophisticated understanding of professional ethics. They are likely to understand that ethical issues require them to weigh and balance the more subtle aspects of a situation.

Figure 2.2, ***Ethical Understanding Over Time***, shows the progression of professional knowledge and skill from novice to maturity.

■ Figure 2.2: Ethical Understanding Over Time

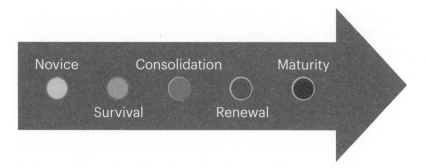

Stages of Moral Development

When you are teaching about ethics, in addition to knowing the stages of professional development, it is helpful to be familiar with **moral development stages** and how they apply to adult learners. The understanding of adult ethical development in this chapter is based to a great extent on the research on moral development conducted by Lawrence Kohlberg and Carol Gilligan. Both described the course of moral development as a set of stages that begin in childhood and become more advanced as individuals move into adulthood. The progression of engagement in moral reasoning through these stages is a result of intellectual ability, increased maturity, and experience.

Individuals at different stages of moral development carry around in their heads different ideas about what is right and what is wrong. As they progress through stages, their views about these things evolve and change. Each stage has a different explanation for why a person should be good and a different approach to reasoning about moral matters.

More than 30 years after they were created, Kohlberg's and Gilligan's theories continue to provide a valuable foundation for teacher educators' understanding of the characteristics of their students' moral reasoning and suggest strategies for supporting their evolving skills in addressing situations that involve ethics.

Moral development stages. A set of stages regarding conceptions of right and wrong that begin in childhood and become more advanced as individuals move into adulthood. The progression through these stages is a result of intellectual ability, increased maturity, and experience.

Kohlberg's Theory of Moral Development

Kohlberg's theory of moral development was built upon Piagetian stage theory, and grew out of 20 years of study during which Kohlberg followed a cohort of male Harvard students. He described the stages of moral development as "systems of thought" that occurred in an ordered "invariant sequence" (Kohlberg & Hersh 1977, 54). Kohlberg proposed three stages of moral development, each of which is divided into two parts.

Figure 2.3: Kohlberg's Stages of Moral Development

Stage	Characteristics	Approach to Moral Decision Making
I: Preconventional morality (characteristic of children ages 2–7)	Thinking is concrete and individual. Children's goal is to avoid punishment by abiding by the rules.	Moral decisions are made either in the individual's best interests or in favor of the most powerful party.
II: Conventional morality (characteristic of children ages 7–12)	Children's goals are to please others by conforming to their expectations, and following the rules that maintain the social order.	Individuals resolve dilemmas by considering existing social rules and by finding resolutions that maintain the social status quo.

Stage	Characteristics	Approach to Moral Decision Making
III: Postconventional morality (also called autonomous, or principled morality) **(adolescent and older, although not everyone reaches this stage)**	Individuals accept rules and laws that are agreed on in society and are based on moral principles. At the highest level, decisions are made based on universal ethical principles and individuals' conscience.	Individuals follow societal expectations. At the highest level, they seek to resolve moral dilemmas by considering universal principles that lie beyond systems of laws and regulations.

Kohlberg believed that there are different ways to discuss morality at each stage, and that dialogical skills develop as a result of having encountered ethical issues in daily life. He believed new forms of thinking were called for in different and more complex situations, and saw moral development as progressing from selfishness to responsibility, and from unquestioning obedience to reasoned, moral decision making. In his view each new stage brings a person a step closer to having the ability to engage in principled moral reasoning. Progression from one stage to the next is based on changes in maturity and cognitive structures, on life experiences, and on being exposed to the thinking of individuals who are at a more advanced stage of moral development. Kohlberg believed it is the disequilibrium caused by new ideas and experiences that promotes higher levels of moral thinking.

Knowledge of Kohlberg's stages helps adult educators to understand that individuals progress through stages of moral development that are characterized by different approaches to moral reasoning. Individuals in the initial stages focus on themselves. As they mature they move toward a morality based on abstract principles.

Gilligan's Theory of Moral Development

Carol Gilligan studied moral development with Kohlberg, but soon identified gaps in his theory that she believed were a result of his work being based on the study of male college students. Gilligan's theory of moral development focuses primarily on relationships and the connections between individuals. Gilligan's feminine perspective of morality sees dilemmas not in terms of rights, as did Kohlberg's, but rather as a matter of balancing conflicting responsibilities. She observed that resolving moral dilemmas requires thinking that is "contextual and narrative rather than formal and abstract" (Gilligan [1982] 1993, 19). Like Kohlberg, Gilligan designates three stages of moral development, but she does not think that individuals move through them in a rigid sequence. She believes that moral growth is a fluid and flexible process (Freeman & Feeney 2016).

Figure 2.4: Gilligan's Stages of Moral Development

Stage	Characteristics	Approach to Moral Decision Making
I: Preconventional morality	Morality focuses on survival.	Individuals focus on their own needs.
II: Conventional morality	Morality involves responsibility for others; self-sacrifice is seen as desirable.	Individuals prioritize their responsibility to care for others, sometimes at the expense of one's own self-interest.
III: Postconventional morality	Morality involves striving to protect oneself and others.	Individuals do not want to hurt themselves or others. Their own needs and those of others are equally important. Avoiding conflict and maintaining relationships are priorities.

Gilligan's teachings are particularly useful for early childhood teacher educators because most teachers of young children are women. Over the years that we have been teaching about professional ethics, we have found that many early childhood educators approach ethical dilemmas in the way that Gilligan describes. They are often so focused on preserving relationships that they need to be reminded that some situations call for making a difficult decision that will not please everyone. Also, we have seen that some early childhood educators are so concerned about meeting the needs of others that they forget to care for themselves.

Moral Reasoning

The ability to understand moral concepts and to engage in increasingly higher levels of moral reflection evolves over time as individuals progress from thinking that is based on direct experience to the ability to think abstractly. As they mature, individuals come to understand moral concepts such as justice, rights, equality, and human welfare.

Researchers investigating the moral development of college students (Levine & Tapp 1977; Torres de Freitas, Kovaleski, & Ferreira de Olviera 2006) found that individuals of the same age may have very different moral capacities, and that many adults never progress beyond Kohlberg's second stage (conventional morality). They point out that the development of skill in moral reasoning is not merely the result of gaining more knowledge, but is instead an ongoing process that involves a sequence of qualitative changes in the way individuals think about moral issues. These changes occur when learners encounter challenging experiences and information that does not fit into their existing worldview. Moral development can continue through adulthood when learners have experiences that challenge their thinking and they are engaged in systematic discussions and guided reflection (Armon 1998; Bebeau 1994). Without such experiences, however, adults may never progress beyond lower levels of ethical reasoning. This points to the importance of focusing on the discussion of ethical issues in the professional development of early childhood educators to support their moral development. Training in ethics needs to give learners opportunities to analyze and resolve relevant ethical dilemmas that expose them to increasingly advanced levels of moral reasoning.

Lisa Johnson, Jonatha Vare, and Rebecca Evers (2013) developed a framework for looking at moral reasoning in teacher candidates that focuses on issues of equity in schools and classrooms. This framework integrates the perspectives of Kohlberg and Gilligan and also incorporates insights from the work of Nel Noddings, a philosopher of moral education who extended Gilligan's ideas to address the importance of care in educational settings.

Figure 2.5: Framework for Understanding Teachers' Stages of Moral Reasoning

Stage	Characteristics
Level I: Personal interest	This stage is characteristic of less experienced (often younger) teachers. The focus is on how teaching–learning situations affect them. In general, they will do what they think they need to do to be successful and gain approval. They are likely to want to apply a code of ethics as if it were an instruction manual that provides an unambiguous "correct" solution to ethical dilemmas.
Level II: Maintaining norms	At this stage, teachers focus on staying in line with the conventional status quo in schools and classrooms. They seek guidance in laws, program policies, and their employer's authority before engaging with ethical analysis. They will also seek answers in a code of ethics not because it is best for them, but because it maintains the established order.
Level III: Principled	In this stage, teachers look at situations in greater depth. They are more likely to focus on universal ethical principles such as justice and equality, and are likely to choose actions based on their conscience. Reasons for rules are important sources of information, but rules are seen as being alterable and relative.

Based on Johnson, Vare, and Evers (2013)

These categories provide another useful lens for examining the characteristics of early childhood educators' engagement with situations that involve ethics. They illustrate differing approaches to using their field's code of professional ethics that reflect different stages of moral development.

Application of Moral Development Stages to Ethics Instruction

Each of the frameworks for looking at moral development discussed in this chapter describes three levels of moral reasoning, and illustrates individuals' progression from decisions based on their own self-interest to a principled approach to morality. Knowledge of these stages can help you to understand how your students approach ethics in their work with young children. An important objective of our field's work in professional ethics is to enhance practitioners' moral development and to support their movement to higher levels of moral reasoning. Our goal is that advanced early childhood educators will engage in postconventional (or principled) moral reasoning, and that they will bring these skills to the ethical dilemmas they face as they work with young children and their families.

The case called "The Birthday Cake" (Feeney & Freeman 2013) presented in the Focus on Ethics column in *Young Children* offers a good example of how stages of professional and moral development can influence educators' perceptions of the kinds of situations they encounter in their work. In this scenario the school has a "no birthday cake" policy. A child whose parent is not proficient in English and has not yet formed a good relationship with the staff arrives at school on her daughter's birthday with a large, elaborately decorated cake to share with the child's class. Opinion about the best course of action for the teacher facing this situation was sharply divided among the early childhood educators who responded to this case.

Quite a few educators, especially inexperienced ones (in the preconventional/personal stage of moral development), maintained adamantly that the rule is the rule and that the teacher should gently and firmly tell the parent that the cake cannot be served.

Those in the conventional morality/maintaining norms stage felt that it was important to explain the health reasons for the policy to the parent and sought to find a way to communicate that the rule is for the good of all. Many of the educators who responded sought out ways to use *ethical finesse* (finding a way to meet the needs of everyone involved without having to make a difficult decision). They tried to find ways to acknowledge the mother's contribution while limiting the amount of cake consumed by the children and following school policies. They suggested actions like having children take a tiny piece of cake, or inviting families to meet in the park for cake after school. This approach illustrates how Gilligan's focus on relationships and Nodding's concept of caring tend to be characteristic of early childhood educators.

The postconventional morality (principled) response in this situation was to prioritize the conflicting obligations to favor preserving a good relationship with the parent above the responsibility to follow all policies to the letter. Teachers at this stage thought the most ethical response was to warmly thank the mother for wanting to celebrate her child's special day and tell her, "We will sing happy birthday and share the cake at lunchtime.

Please stay and join us." They also realized that the policy should be examined, and if it were to stay in place it needed to be communicated more effectively to all families.

When you understand that this range of responses is a function of the teachers' stages of moral development, you can help them examine their assumptions and think about alternatives. It is possible to help teachers learn to think more abstractly and to achieve a higher level of moral reasoning, but the process takes time and requires a skilled adult educator. In general, age, maturity, education, and professional experience increase the likelihood that a teacher will be able to engage in the kind of complex thinking that characterizes the postconventional (principled) stage of ethical reasoning. This is often, but not always, the case.

Effective adult educators take the learner's characteristics into account as they decide which activities and teaching strategies will best fit their needs and interests. The chapters that follow introduce instructional strategies for teaching professional ethics, including how they can be adapted to different groups of learners. Chapter 5 contains more information about how to support the development of higher levels of ethical reasoning.

Three

Teaching About Morality and Ethics

Early childhood practitioners who have had little or no background in professional ethics will benefit from learning experiences that help them develop the necessary vocabulary and begin to learn about personal and professional values and ethics. Those who have some previous knowledge will be ready to build on their work experience and on what they have already learned.

This chapter explores ways that you can help participants in a course or workshop to reflect on their personal values and morality and to understand how these are similar to, or different from, the professional values and ethics of the field.

Terminology

Definitions of terms that are frequently used when talking about morality and ethics are listed below. They are also in the glossary in this book and in the NAEYC Code of Ethical Conduct, and are discussed in *Ethics and the Early Childhood Educator*. These terms are foundational for understanding this subject. It is important that you begin conversations about morality and ethics with definitions of these terms as they are used when discussing professional ethics.

Note: Use the information in this chapter to give participants a background in morality and professional ethics or, more specifically, to teach participants about Chapter 1, "An Introduction to Morality and Ethics," in *Ethics and the Early Childhood Educator*.

Code of ethics. Defines the core values of the field and provides guidance for what professionals should do when they encounter conflicting obligations or responsibilities in their work.

Core values. Commitments held by a profession that are consciously and knowingly embraced by its practitioners because they make a contribution to society. There is a difference between personal values and the core values of a profession.

Ethical dilemma. A moral conflict that involves determining appropriate conduct when an individual faces conflicting professional values and responsibilities. (A dilemma has two defensible resolutions.)

Ethical responsibilities. (Also referred to as *professional responsibilities*.) Behaviors that one must or must not engage in. Ethical responsibilities are clear-cut and are spelled out in the Code of Ethical Conduct.

Ethics. The study of right and wrong, or duty and obligation, that involves critical reflection on morality and the ability to make choices between values and the examination of the moral dimensions of relationships.

Morality. People's views of what is good, right, and proper; their beliefs about their obligations; and their ideas about how they should behave.

Professional ethics. The moral commitments of a profession that involve moral reflection that extends and enhances the personal morality practitioners bring to their work, that concern actions of right and wrong in the workplace, and that help individuals resolve moral dilemmas they encounter in their work.

Values. Qualities or principles that individuals believe to be desirable or worthwhile and that they prize for themselves, for others, and for the world in which they live.

A note about terminology. The terms *morality* and *ethics* are often used interchangeably. In this book the term *morality* refers to personal value choices and the term *ethics* refers to professional values and responsibilities.

Awareness of Ethical Issues

You can make the topic of ethics real and meaningful by introducing students to some of the kinds of ethical issues teachers of young children are likely to encounter in their work. Ethical issues are situations that involve determining what is right and wrong, rights and responsibilities, and human welfare. Class discussions might reveal that students have wondered how they should handle the 4-year-old who is so rough that he hurts other children, how they should respond when the father of a 2-year-old demands to know

How to Identify Activities for Different Learners

Chapters 1, 3, 4, and 5 have activities that are designed to help students get to know each other and learn about and apply the NAEYC Code of Ethical Conduct. Each activity is identified as Icebreaker (Introductory), Beginning, Intermediate, or Advanced. The Icebreaker activities in Chapter 1 are designed to help participants get to know each other. Beginning activities are designed to promote understanding of basic concepts related to ethics and introduce the Code. Intermediate activities expand on basic knowledge of the Code. Advanced activities involve application and are for those who are acquainted with the Code and familiar with the process of ethical analysis.

who had bitten his toddler, or how they might approach a teacher who is routinely harsh and disrespectful when disciplining kindergartners.

Guiding students through an exploration of these issues can help them understand why their personal and idiosyncratic values are not sufficient to guide their actions in a professional setting. Over time they will come to see the value of a code that can guide them toward a response that is right, fair, and just, in addition to being based on standards that provide a shared common ground for educators who strive to do the right thing for children and families. They will also learn that the use of a code can back them up when they take an unpopular moral stand, such as respectfully refusing to identify the child who had bitten the toddler whose father was upset.

Activities Related to Awareness of Ethical Issues

Activity 3.1: Reflection on Situations That Involve Ethics (Beginning)

Have participants think about and then write or discuss their responses to the following ethical issues or other issues that are frequently found in early childhood programs.

- It has been raining for days. The children are restless, and you are having a hard time helping them stay busy inside. A teacher from another class offers to loan you a new, full-length animated superhero video.
- The families of the children in your class want you to teach academic skills to 4-year-olds using large group, primarily lecture-and-drill methods, instead of providing the developmentally appropriate hands-on activities you have learned are best for young children.

Reflection: Have you encountered problems like these? Where did you turn for help? What would you say to a friend or colleague who is facing one of these situations and asks for your advice? (Feeney, Freeman, & Pizzolongo 2012, 2)

Activity 3.2: Reflection on Differing Viewpoints (Beginning)

Have participants think about and then write or discuss their responses to the following reflection about colleagues having different solutions to workplace problems.

Reflection: Have you ever found yourself and a colleague coming up with very different solutions to the same workplace problem? How did you decide what to do? Where did you turn for help? What did you learn from the experience? (Feeney, Freeman, & Pizzolongo 2012, 3).

Personal Values and Morality

Everyone who works with young children brings to the workplace their own personal values and morality that they have acquired from their families, religious traditions, and communities. This personal morality is an essential foundation for working with young children, but it varies greatly between individuals and communities, making a unified approach to **moral behavior** in early childhood programs practically impossible.

Moral behavior. Behaving in ways that reflect standards of morality.

When working with beginners or students who have not been exposed to instruction in ethics, a good place to start is to ask them to identify the personal values they bring to their work. They may find that these beliefs are so natural and instinctive they have difficulty putting them into words or explaining them to classmates whose early experiences, culture, and family backgrounds are very different from their own. You might also ask students to consider the source of some of their personal values, to prioritize these values, or to compare some of their strongly held beliefs with those of their classmates to highlight the fact that the field welcomes individuals with a wide range of beliefs about personal issues that do not relate directly to working with children and families.

Activities That Focus on Personal Values and Morality

Professional values and ethics are, to a large extent, an extension of *personal* values and morality. Engaging in activities that focus on personal values allows participants to see that ethics is not terrifyingly abstract and is grounded in their lives.

Activity 3.3: Reflection on Personal Values (Beginning)

Have participants think about and then write or discuss their responses to the following reflection about personal values.

Reflection: Identify some personal values that have led you to choose a career working with young children. Think of some things you do with children and families that reflect these values. Think about a teacher who has positively influenced your life. What personal values did that teacher demonstrate? (Feeney, Freeman, & Pizzolongo 2012, 5)

Activity 3.4: Reflection on Personal Morality (Beginning)

Have participants think about and then write or discuss their responses to the following reflection about personal morality.

Reflection: What are some of your strongly held ideas about morality? Where or from whom do you think you acquired them? Reflect on the experiences in your life that led you to develop these views of morality. (Feeney, Freeman, & Pizzolongo 2012, 5)

Activity 3.5: My Gift to Children (Beginning)

Ask participants to think about the children with whom they work and the one special gift they wish they could give each child. Explain that the gift should be something intangible (i.e., not a toy, object, or resource such as money) they would like children to know, believe in, or be able to do.

Provide participants with a sheet of paper titled "My Gift to Children" (see Activity 3.5 on page 98 in the Appendix) above a simple drawing of a box. Ask participants to write a description of the gift they envision and decorate the box using markers or crayons.

When all participants have finished their drawings, ask them to share their work with a partner or with the whole group. If the setting allows, post the drawings on the walls. Lead a discussion that helps the participants reach the following conclusions:

- Each gift is important.
- Each individual has values that influence the gift she or he wishes to give children.
- There are similarities and differences in what we value for children.

Adapted by permission from S. Nolte, *PACE (Professional and Career Education for Early Childhood) Training Manual for ED 140,* rev. ed. (Honolulu: Honolulu Community College, 1998).

Activity 3.6: The Wall of Personal Values (Beginning)

This activity requires a room in which the furniture is arranged so that participants are able to walk from one side of the room to the other. Label opposite walls of the room with signs saying **Strongly Agree** and **Strongly Disagree.** Explain to the participants that the width of the room represents a continuum of personal opinion.

Read aloud several statements that reflect values. For each statement, ask participants to walk to a place along the continuum that best represents the extent to which they agree or disagree. Figure 3.1, **_Personal Values Statements_**, provides some examples of statements you could use.

Figure 3.1. Personal Values Statements

- It is better to do good than to be wealthy.
- It is more important to be smart than to be good or moral.
- It is okay to lie under certain circumstances.
- Following your own conscience is more important than doing what others want you to do.
- It is important to follow the law even if you disagree with it.
- Family responsibilities are more important than responsibilities to yourself or your employer.
- It would be okay to steal if your family really needed something.
- As a society, we have the responsibility to make sure that all peoples' basic needs are met.
- People need formal religious institutions to help them determine what is right and wrong.
- No price is too great to preserve our environment.

Note: Be cautious about using topics that are very controversial or that might upset some participants (e.g., abortion or the death penalty). The purpose of this activity is to emphasize that professional colleagues can have a range of values, not to generate debate.

Start with statements that represent perspectives on personal values and morality that are likely to cause little conflict or difference. Gradually move to statements that are likely to illustrate more differences of opinion. As the activity progresses, note any body language that suggests discomfort. Although some discomfort is useful, too much may prevent participants from engaging in other activities.

After participants have responded to a few personal values statements, spend some time discussing what you found. Comment that there were similarities and differences within the group, and there may have been some surprises when individuals discovered some people held views that were quite different from their own.

Ask the group to discuss the experience—what they had expected and what they found surprising. Note that all of the sample statements reflect values. Ask participants, "Is it possible for two people to be good professionals even if they have very different values? Why?"

Variation 1 on The Wall of Personal Values (Beginning)

Instead of having participants physically moving to a position of agreement/disagreement, give them a worksheet that contains personal value statements and have them mark their position along each continuum. In small groups have them compare the positions that individuals take. The worksheet for Variation 1 on The Wall of Personal Values: Personal Values Continua is on page 99 of the Appendix.

Variation 2 on The Wall of Personal Values (Beginning)

Ask participants to create their own values statements. Then repeat the process. Use the Personal Values Continua worksheet from the previous activity.

Activity 3.7: Sources of Values (Beginning)

Ask participants to make a list of 10 to 15 ideals, principles, qualities, accomplishments, or activities that they value highly. If you wish, provide a prepared list similar to Activity 3.7: Sources of Values found on page 100 of the Appendix. Have participants check, add, or eliminate values. When the lists are finished, ask them to indicate the source (person or people, institution or experience) for each value in their own lives.

With the whole group, compile a list of the sources of personal values and discuss why individuals' values may be different.

Variation on Sources of Values (Beginning)

Add a third column labeled *Action* to participants' lists. Have them write an action they take in their lives that grows out of each value. Working in pairs or all together in the larger group, discuss how values influence their lives and work.

Activity 3.8: Values Auction (Beginning)

Create a collection of values signs (see Activity 3.8 on page 101 of the Appendix for 35 signs you can duplicate). Give each participant $100 in play money (an assortment of $1, $5, $10, and $20 bills) and show them the available values signs. To begin the auction, explain that participants can bid on the values that you have for sale. Hold up one value card at a time (use all 35 value signs or select the ones that reflect the values of the participants). Participants bid on values, and the auctioneer awards each one to the highest bidder. You can play until all the values have been sold or everyone runs out of money.

When the auction concludes, ask the participants what they noticed about themselves during the bidding and how strongly they felt about different values. Next, ask the group what differences they noticed in participants' bidding and buying. Lead a discussion that suggests that people have different values, or that they value some things more highly than others. You might discuss why people have such different values.

Activity 3.9: Values Sort (Beginning)

The Values Sort activity is similar to the Values Auction activity. It is appropriate when participants are more reserved or likely to be uncomfortable with the competition that is part of the Values Auction. Create a collection of values cards (using the same 35 values cards from the Values Auction). Make enough so there is one set for each participant. It helps to print sets of cards on different colors of paper. That makes it possible for you to keep sets separate and to avoid duplications or omissions. Sometimes this activity is more powerful because participants have to handle the cards. An alternative to making many sets of cards is to give each participant a sheet of paper with a list of the 35 values on the values signs (see Activity 3.8 and 3.9 on pages 102–105 in the Appendix).

To begin, explain that each person must select 10 values from the 35. Encourage participants to read quietly, and to thoughtfully consider which 10 are most important to them and discard the rest (or cross them off if you are using a list). Discarding values can be difficult, but is an important part of the activity. Finally, ask participants to choose from these 10 the five that are most highly prized.

Ask participants to join with three others (if possible, people they do not know well) and sit together. Invite groups to compare and discuss their choices, talk about what led them to make those choices, and share how it felt to make those choices. You could ask them to collaborate to create a list of five or 10 that reflect their agreed-upon values. They may

Teaching the NAEYC Code of Ethical Conduct

discover how difficult it can be to reach consensus. Summarize the experience by noting that values are very personal, very intense, and hard to let go of. You can say that we are often not aware of how our values differ from those of other people. To close the activity, ask participants to go back to the values they chose and identify their origins (family, friends, colleagues, society, religious community, etc.)

Variation on Values Sort (Beginning)

Give each participant 15 values cards. After they have put them in order of their importance, ask participants to work in pairs to create a prioritized list of five values they can agree on. Those two participants can then join with another pair of participants so that four are working together to develop a consensus list of prioritized values. They soon come to appreciate the diverse perspectives that early childhood educators bring to their work.

Activity 3.10: Values Poem (Beginning)

Following the Values Sort activity, have participants choose one of their top five values as the basis for a poem with the following format. Demonstrate using a model, such as the one given here.

Health
(value)

Good-Bad
(two words to describe the value)

breathing, sensing, living
(three action words ending in ING)

Life is nothing without it!
(a sentence)

Essential!
(an impact word)

You might ask the students to share their poems with a partner or with the group, and discuss similarities and differences in what they chose to write about and how it felt to write about their deeply held values.

Activity 3.11: What Would You Do? (Beginning)

Ask participants to reflect on what they would do in a variety of situations involving personal moral choices. In small groups, have them explain what they would do and why, and explain what influences in their lives led them to believe their choices are morally defensible. Ask them to list the personal values that influenced their choices. Some sample situations you might read to the group appear in Figure 3.2.

◾ Figure 3.2: What Would You Do? Scenarios

The mom-and-pop store. You go to a neighborhood mom-and-pop grocery and give a $10 bill for a $3.50 purchase. You take your change and walk out. Outside the store you realize that the cashier has given you change for $20. What would you do?

The chain discount store. You go to an outlet of a nationwide chain discount store and use a charge card to pay. When you get your credit card bill, you realize that you were charged $9.95 for an item that cost $39.95. What would you do?

The towel. You are staying in a hotel that has nice, thick towels. On the day you plan to leave, you go for a swim and return to your room to pack. Your bathing suit is wet, and there are no plastic bags. If you don't wrap your bathing suit in something, you will ruin your clothes. What would you do?

The water playground. Your friend is the lifeguard at an exclusive club that has an elaborate water playground. Members are identified in the water with a special bracelet they wear. Your friend offers to give you a bracelet so that you can go any time you want. What would you do?

The special party. The day of the event is approaching. You accept an invitation from someone who is romantically interested in you, even though you're really not interested. The next day the person you most wish would ask you out invites you to the party. What would you do?

The dented fender. You're backing your car out of a tight space in a parking garage. You hear a crunch and realize that you have hit the car next to you. You get out and see that there is a small dent in the side of the brand-new car. No one saw you. What would you do?

Teaching the NAEYC Code of Ethical Conduct

Activity 3.12: Choosing What's Right (Beginning)

Using the dilemmas described in Figure 3.3, give pairs of participants matched statements that describe two opposing points of view, each of which could be justified as being right. Ask the first person to share and justify her or his position for a minute or two, then switch and have the other partner give a justification for the opposing viewpoint. Set a timer to be sure both people have the same amount of time to make their cases. Continue with several pairs of statements.

Bring the pairs together in the larger group and invite them to discuss what this experience has taught them about moral dilemmas. Introduce the idea that right-versus-wrong choices (responsibilities versus temptations) are very different from right-versus-right choices (dilemmas).

Figure 3.3: Choosing What's Right Dilemmas

The right thing to do is to support logging of old growth forest to provide jobs in an economically depressed area.	The right thing to do is to oppose the logging of old growth forest in order to preserve air quality, the environment, and animal habitats.
The right thing to do is to leave natural areas undeveloped and unspoiled.	The right thing to do is develop some natural areas to provide needed housing and commercial centers.
The right thing to do is to group high-performing students together to give them special educational opportunities to ensure they reach their potential.	The right thing to do is to group students so there are mixed abilities in all classes so they learn from each other and all have the same opportunities.
The right thing to do is to ensure that students admitted to college represent a wide range of ethnicities.	The right thing to do is to base college admissions only on students' past performance.
The right thing to do is to require that all children be fully immunized before they enroll in school.	The right thing to do is to allow families to make the decision about whether or not to immunize their children.
The right thing to do is to be honest even if it might hurt another person's feelings.	The right thing to do is to avoid hurting other people's feelings even if it means occasionally being dishonest.
The right thing to do is to seek the best paying job available in order to provide well for one's family even if it means compromising principles and beliefs.	The right thing to do is to seek a job that provides the best opportunity to make a contribution to others.

Based on R.M. Kidder (2009)

Activity 3.13: Children's Literature Connections (Beginning)

We often begin or bring closure to a session by reading a children's book that relates to or illuminates the session's topic. When teaching about morality and ethics, we have read

Red Is Best, by Kathy Stinson, to discuss how personal preferences are different from values

Bread and Jam for Frances, by Russell Hoban, which illustrates Frances' preference (for bread and jam) as well as her parents' values (a balanced and varied diet)

The Empty Pot, by Demi, to illustrate personal morality

Song for the Ancient Forest, by Nancy Luenn, as an example of a societal ethical dilemma

Professional Values and Ethics

Personal values and morality form a necessary foundation for an individual's professional practice, but they need to be complemented with professional values and standards of ethical behavior in order for members of a profession to be able to speak with one voice about their professional responsibilities. A code of professional ethics reflects the collective wisdom of a field. It is based on systematic reflection on moral beliefs and obligations that provide a unified approach to professional ethical behavior. The professional commitments that people have are different than personal ones, though both are important.

What Is a Profession?

A *profession* is an occupation whose members provide an essential service to society. Because professionals do work that is important to society, every profession needs to assure the public that its members are committed to honoring the best interests of those they serve. The requirement for ethical behavior that is set out in a code of ethics is a hallmark of every profession. The educator who works with young children has a particularly strong obligation to do what is right, since the potential benefits and the potential harm they can do are so great. Those who work with children need to understand their ethical responsibilities and how to constructively address the ethical issues they encounter every day.

Considering the criteria that are used to determine if an occupation is a profession, the field of early childhood education has not yet achieved full professional status in the eyes of our society. The field meets some of the criteria that are used to recognize professional status very well—commitment to a significant social value, altruism (unselfish dedication), and a code of ethics (though it is not enforced). But the field is still a long way from achieving others (lengthy training, high standards for admission, autonomy).

Note: "An Introduction to Morality and Ethics," Chapter 1 of *Ethics and the Early Childhood Educator,* includes an excellent discussion of the professional status of early childhood education.

The case can be made that at this time in its history, the field is working toward professional status and that it can be best described as an emerging profession. Though early childhood educators may not be recognized as "true" professionals, they perform a significant service to society as they work with children at a critical stage in the life cycle. Because of the power they have in children's lives, it is imperative that they work to achieve the ideals of professions that include dedication to service, priority to the interests of those they serve, standards of competence, and integrity. You can emphasize in your teaching that regardless of the professional status of the field, early childhood educators should have a strong moral commitment to children.

Professional Values and Professionalism Activities

Individuals' awareness of personal values and morals can lead them toward an understanding of professional values. The following activities are designed to help adult learners develop an understanding of the characteristics of a profession, become aware of the professional values of early childhood education, and see how professional values differ from personal values.

Activity 3.14: The Wall of Professional Values (Beginning)

This activity is closely related to Activity 3.6: The Wall of Personal Values, described on page 28. It can be used as a follow-up to that activity. It requires a room in which the furniture is arranged so that participants are able to walk from one side of the room to the other. Label opposite walls of the room with signs saying **Strongly Agree** and **Strongly Disagree.** Explain to the participants that the width of the room represents a continuum of personal opinion about *professional* values. Read statements to the group that reflect professional values and ask participants to walk to the place along the continuum between the walls that best represents their viewpoint. Figure 3.4 has examples of statements you might use.

◢ Figure 3.4: Professional Values Statements

- A teacher's most important task is to help children feel good about themselves.
- Children who attend preschool and kindergarten should learn the discipline that they will need later in school.
- Children won't learn unless the teacher tells them what to do.
- Development of intellectual skills is the most important task of an early childhood program.
- Given enough time and equipment, children will learn all they need without traditional, intentional teaching.
- Children should be allowed to play in school.
- Families should not be allowed to interfere in their child's learning at school.
- To be fair, all children should be treated the same way in school.
- It is important for teachers to be responsive to the individual needs and interests of all children.
- It is appropriate for educators to use rewards to help change children's behaviors.
- Early childhood curricula should be based on what children will need to know later in school.
- Children who misbehave should not be allowed special privileges.
- It is important for children [choose an age group] to learn to color within and cut on the lines, write neatly, stand in line, and use proper punctuation.

Variation on The Wall of Professional Values (Beginning)

Instead of having participants physically move to locations between the walls that represent their opinions, have them mark their positions on paper (see Activity 3.14, Professional Values Continua, on page 106 of the Appendix). With a partner or in small groups, individuals may compare and discuss their responses.

Teaching the NAEYC Code of Ethical Conduct

Activity 3.15: Reflect on Professional Values (Beginning)

Using the following reflection, have participants form small groups and work on lists of values they think that *all* early childhood educators should hold.

> *Reflection:* Brainstorm a list of values that you think all early childhood educators should hold. (If possible, do this activity with one or two colleagues or classmates.) Compare your list to the list of Core Values in the NAEYC Code of Ethical Conduct. Consider why these lists are similar to each other or different. (Feeney, Freeman, & Pizzolongo 2012, 8)

After the small groups brainstorm, bring the whole group together to look at the lists and discuss how they are similar to or different from each others'. Compare them to NAEYC's Core Values and explain that a profession's core values form a foundation for its code of ethics. Read the Core Values from the NAEYC Code out loud and invite the participants to reflect silently on their personal reaction and commitment to each one.

Activity 3.16: Is It a Profession? (Beginning)

Ask participants to name two or three jobs they regard as professions. If they need help, give them some examples of occupations such as politician, real estate agent, engineer, secretary, CEO of a large company, doctor, maintenance worker, nurse, cook at a fast food restaurant, lawyer, and librarian. Participants are likely to express a variety of opinions. Some may believe that anyone who gets paid to work or who receives a high salary is a professional, and others may say that only certain highly trained individuals deserve professional status.

Explain that you are looking for occupations that everyone agrees are professions. Once the group has agreed upon this list, form small groups and ask them to brainstorm characteristics that are shared by these occupations.

When the groups report back, share their lists of characteristics and compare them to the list "Criteria for Professional Status" (see Activity 3.16 on page 107 of the Appendix), which was developed by studying the literature describing professions. Have them consider if the occupations they identify as professions actually do meet the criteria for professional status.

Activity 3.17: Assessing Our Professionalism (Beginning)

This activity is a good way to illustrate the professional status of the field of early childhood education. Before implementing it, be sure to read the section "What Is a Profession?" on pages 6–8 in *Ethics and the Early Childhood Educator*. Explain to participants that they are going to work together to assess the professional status of early childhood education. You can pass out the "Criteria for Professional Status," found in Activity 3.16 on page 107 in the Appendix.

Tell the participants that they can award up to 10 points for each criteria for a total maximum of 80 points. Ask them to propose points for each criterion, and ask them to explain their justification to the group for awarding this number. Use the "Assessing Our Professionalism Scoring Sheet" (Activity 3.17 on page 108 in the Appendix) to record the number of points awarded for each criterion. Explain that you will serve as moderator and make the final decision if there is a disagreement. If someone says that a criterion deserves 2 points and another thinks that it should be 6, you can pick a middle position or the one that you think best reflects the status of the field of early childhood education. You can also override a number if you think it is too high or too low.

Note: You may find that participants propose that early childhood education receive 10 points for having a code of ethics. Sadly, that is not warranted because the NAEYC Code is not enforced by a professional association as are the codes of universally recognized professions such as medicine and law. You can point out that the use of the NAEYC Code is voluntary, though it is widely disseminated and used.

After the group has scored each criterion, total the points. Scores for the early childhood education field often range from 40–60, depending on how rigorous the participants choose to be. Summarize participants' judgments by saying something like, "We can see from this activity that early childhood education is an occupation that is striving to achieve professional status. We aren't there yet, but we are making progress. We meet some criteria admirably (serving a significant social value, altruism), but we are quite far from achieving the criteria of autonomy and rigorous requirements for entry." Point out that even if our field is not fully recognized as a profession, we make a significant contribution to our society, and because we work with children at such a critical period in the life cycle, it is imperative that we uphold high standards of professional behavior.

The activities that follow are designed to help participants build their awareness of ethics and knowledge about ethical codes.

Activity 3.18: Ethics in the News, in the Comics (Beginning)

Whether you're teaching a workshop or a course, you can help participants realize that issues of morality and ethics come up often in everyday life. An effective way to begin an introductory workshop or conference session is by sharing newspaper headlines or comics related to ethics and morality. These don't have to relate to education, schools, or teaching. Whatever the specific topic, newspaper stories help participants realize that ethics is a topic that affects all parts of our lives.

In order to do this you need a collection of ethics-related headlines and cartoons. Start your collection by keeping an eye out for headlines and relevant comic strips in your local newspaper.

Classic Peanuts, Doonesbury, The Family Circus, and others often address values, morals, and ethics. Headlines and comic strips help an audience appreciate the ethical dimensions of their everyday lives.

Activity 3.19: Brainstorming—Why a Code of Ethics? (Beginning)

Why is it important for a profession to have a code of ethics? Divide participants into small groups to brainstorm some answers to this question. Have the groups report back and compare their responses. Emphasize the following points, if students have addressed them. Add any that they didn't mention.

- Professionals are doing a job that is essential to the society.
- Professionals are the only ones who can do a particular job.
- Professionals monitor themselves (no one else tells them what to do).

It is essential, therefore, that a profession as a whole agrees that its members will conduct themselves according to high moral standards.

Points to Emphasize in Your Teaching

- While personal values and morality are important, they cannot be the sole guide for professional behavior. They need to be supplemented with professional values and standards of ethical behavior.
- There is a fundamental difference between personal morality and professional ethics.
- Like individuals, professions have distinctive values and ethics.
- Ethical standards are not statements of taste or preference, nor are they the same as laws.
- A code of ethics is an important feature of every profession. It codifies professional values and standards, spells out moral responsibilities to society, and provides guidelines for moral behavior.
- Professional ethical commitments described in the NAEYC Code of Ethical Conduct help to unify our field because they apply to everyone who works with young children.
- Because the work we do is so important, it is essential that early childhood educators have a moral commitment to children—and understand that a code of ethics can help us to know and act on that commitment.

Four

Teaching the Code of Ethical Conduct

Given the role of ethics in professions and the importance of the work that early childhood educators do, it is not surprising that NAEYC, the largest professional association of early childhood educators in the United States, has a strong commitment to ethical practice and a widely known and used Code of Ethical Conduct. The NAEYC Code can be viewed as the moral compass for the work of early childhood educators, especially since there is so little else that is consistent or standardized in our field.

Learning about the NAEYC Code is an essential component of the study of professional ethics in early childhood education. It is included in professional standards for NAEYC Accreditation for programs serving young children, as well as in postsecondary programs preparing teachers to work with young children (CAEP 2013; CAEP 2014; NAEYC 2012; NAEYC 2015). Many individuals and programs have committed to making it foundational in their practice.

Note: Use the information in this chapter to teach participants about the NAEYC Code of Ethical Conduct, or more specifically, about Chapter 2, "The NAEYC Code of Ethical Conduct," in *Ethics and the Early Childhood Educator*.

Why Is a Code of Ethics Important?

A code of ethics is important in our field, and it is essential for early childhood educators to have, know, and honor a code. The two most important reasons for early childhood education to have a code of ethics are these:

1. Early childhood educators need to behave ethically on behalf of young children because they can do great good and also great harm.
2. Early childhood educators have obligations to a number of different constituencies—children, families, colleagues, administrators, communities, agencies, and policy makers. The code can provide guidance in navigating obligations to each of these groups, which that are sometimes in conflict.

The code also provides support for behaving ethically when there is pressure or temptation to do what is easiest or what is popular. And it helps to enhance respect for the field because letting others know our commitment to ethical standards enhances the field's credibility and professionalism.

Note: "The NAEYC Code of Ethical Conduct," Chapter 2 of *Ethics and the Early Childhood Educator*, includes sections on why a code of ethics is important for early childhood educators; a history of the development of the Code; a description of its organization; and discussion of revisions, enforcement, and endorsements by other professional groups. If you are giving a one-time workshop or class session for teachers who are new to the field, or those receiving a brief overview, a good place to begin is with an introduction to the Code, its importance, how it is structured, and how it can be used to guide ethical decision making. You may want to touch only lightly or skip sections on history, revision, endorsement, and enforcement. This information might be included in trainings for experienced educators and those in degree programs, but may not be very relevant to beginners. If you are conducting a course or series of non-introductory workshops, we strongly recommend that you have students read the Code and "The NAEYC Code of Ethical Conduct," Chapter 2 in *Ethics and the Early Childhood Educator*, before beginning your sessions.

Organization of the Code

If you are offering a one-time workshop or class session for teachers who are new to the field, or for those receiving a brief overview, you might begin by discussing how the Code is structured and how it can be used to guide ethical decision making. Be sure that everyone in your workshop or class has a copy of the Code. You might have copies of the brochure on hand to give to students because they are easy to handle and refer to. If you don't have brochures, you can download the Code from the NAEYC website and make copies for participants.

Begin the study of the Code by discussing the Core Values that provide its foundation. You might have already asked students individually or in small groups to brainstorm a list of what they believe to be the field's most important values, the principles upon which all early childhood educators can agree. If you haven't already done that activity as part of your overview of ethics and morality, it is a good way to introduce the NAEYC Code. After students have compiled a list, you can have them compare their list with the Core Values identified in the NAEYC Code. It can be surprising how similar these are. Additional activities for beginners to help them get to know the Code include

- Rephrasing its items or reassembling copies of the Code that have been cut apart (with identifying items removed).

Teaching the NAEYC Code of Ethical Conduct

- Looking at how it is organized. Point out that it is divided into four sections—early childhood educators' ethical responsibilities to children, to families, to colleagues, and to community and society. Show that each of these sections is divided into Ideals (ideal or exemplary professional behavior) and Principles (rules of professional conduct that clearly state practices that are required and those that are prohibited).

After students have developed some familiarity with the content and organization of the Code, they are ready to learn how it can guide their efforts to deal with the ethical issues they encounter in their work. It is important to help them understand that the Code is not an instruction manual like a cookbook, but a tool to guide ethical decision making. As students grapple with realistic scenarios, it may be helpful to remind them that "doing ethics . . . is nothing more than *systematic critical reflection about [their] obligations*" (emphasis in the original) (Kipnis 1987, 27), and that a code of ethics provides a framework for this reflection.

Beginners who are not yet facing ethical issues in the classroom may benefit from activities that give them opportunities to read the Code and see examples of how it can help them to make future difficult decisions. (See the activities that follow.) An effective way to do this is to play the Is It Ethical? game. It presents short scenarios, describes the way the early childhood educator in the situation chose to respond, and asks "Is it ethical?" Students then decide if they think this response was *ethical* (E) or *not ethical* (NE) and refer to specific items in the Code to justify their decision. Chapter 5 discusses how adult educators can help students learn to address real-life ethical dilemmas and how to support students in developing higher levels of moral reasoning.

How to Identify Activities for Different Learners

Chapters 1, 3, 4, and 5 have activities that are designed to help students get to know each other and learn about and apply the NAEYC Code of Ethical Conduct. Each activity is identified as Icebreaker (Introductory), Beginning, Intermediate, or Advanced. The Icebreaker activities in Chapter 1 are designed to help participants get to know each other. Beginning activities are designed to promote understanding of basic concepts related to ethics and introduce the Code. Intermediate activities expand on basic knowledge of the Code. Advanced activities involve application and are for those who are acquainted with the Code and familiar with the process of ethical analysis.

NAEYC Code Activities

The following activities will help participants in a course or workshop to understand how the Code is organized, how it can be used, and why it is important.

Activity 4.1: Your Values, the Code's Values (Beginning)

In this activity students compare the list of professional values that they developed (in Activity 3.15: Reflect on Professional Values on page 37) with the Core Values from the NAEYC Code. Have students take out the list of Core Values that they developed. (If you have not already had students do this activity, have them do it before taking this next step.)

- Have them go through the list of core values they developed to see if and how they align with the Core Values in the NAEYC Code.
- Make a note of any values that aren't included in the Code, and have students discuss why they think they aren't there.
- Have students think about whether the items they suggested are values or responsibilities.
- Discuss what they notice about the similarities and differences between the two lists.

Activity 4.2: In Other Words (Beginning)

If you are doing this activity with a group that meets regularly, assign a read-through of the Code as homework.

- Divide participants into small groups of two to six individuals. Assign each small group the task of reading one section of Principles from the Code. "Ethical Responsibilities to Children" may be broken down into two parts, P-1.1 to P-1.6 and P-1.7 to P-1.11. "Ethical Responsibilities to Families" may be broken down into two parts, P-2.1 to P-2.8 and P-2.9 to P-2.15. "Ethical Responsibilities to Colleagues" may be broken down by sections on coworkers, employers, and employees. "Ethical Responsibilities to Community and Society" may be broken down into two parts, P-4.1 to P-4.6 and P-4.7 to P-4.13.
- Give chart paper and a set of colored markers to each small group. In advance, write at the top of the sheets of chart paper, "Our responsibilities to (children, families, etc.) are to…"
- Explain that each group is to summarize in one to three sentences the big ideas for its section of the Code. Remind the groups to focus on the ethical Principles (the musts and must nots) rather than the Ideals (the aspirations). When the groups have completed that task, ask each group to use the chart paper and markers to write and illustrate its sentences on chart paper and post them on the walls or bulletin boards of the room.
- When all the posters are up, walk through the work that has been done, pointing out that each section of the Code has some important ideas that are guiding principles for

our work with children. Be sure to point to Principle 1.1 as the overriding Principle of our work with children.

It may be too much of a challenge for students to understand the responsibilities we have to the multiple clients identified in the Code. If you sense that the participants you are working with would benefit from a more focused and less comprehensive approach, concentrate on just one section at a time.

- Select one section that seems most relevant to the group: responsibilities to children, families, colleagues, or community and society.
- Download the Code from NAEYC's website. Cut it apart and distribute a section of it to participants, and then try Activity 4.2: In Other Words, thus limiting your focus.

Activity 4.3: Ethical Code Puzzle (Beginning)

A puzzle can encourage participants to actually read the words of the Code. It helps participants see the Code as a whole, like a completed jigsaw puzzle.

To make the puzzle, follow these steps:

- Print out a copy of the Code of Ethical Conduct, beginning with Section 1.
- Remove the titles and numbers from all the sections so that all you have left is the written text.
- Make a copy of the altered Code for each group of participants, and cut it apart so that each group has a set of pieces that includes the following:
    1. Each of the "Ethical Responsibilities" sections with titles removed
    2. All the "Ideals" sections with the numbers removed and cut into two or more segments
    3. All the "Principles" sections with the numbers removed and cut into two or more segments

To assemble the puzzle, follow these steps:

- Divide participants into small groups.
- Have participants sort the pieces of the puzzle into piles that go together.
- Give groups labels with the titles from the Code ("Section 1: Ethical Responsibilities to Children," etc.) and ask them to place the label with the correct pile.

Simplify the activity by focusing on one section of the Code at a time.

Activity 4.4: In My Experience (Beginning)

In this activity, small groups of participants share and discuss their real-life experiences related to a single ethical principle. By focusing in this way, participants find relevance that may be lost in trying to decipher the entire Code.

Preparation

- Make a copy of the NAEYC Code. Cut out the individual Principles.
- Place several Principles (these need not be related or from the same section of the Code) in an envelope on a table for a small group of participants. Be sure to include at least one Principle that relates to a common situation (e.g., divorce—P-2.14; suspected child abuse—P-1.9; or concerns about a coworker—P-3A.2), as well as Principles related to less frequently encountered situations.

What You Do

- Have participants work in small groups. Ask a member of each group to open the envelope, select a Principle, and read it aloud to the group.
- Explain that the group's task is to think of and discuss situations the members have encountered in which they have applied this Principle, or in which knowledge of this Principle would have helped them to better address the situation.
- Explain that if no member of the small group has had a related real-life experience, the group should move on to the next Principle.
- Ask each small group to briefly report back—you may wish to focus on Principles from one section of the Code at a time.
- As groups report back, encourage them to make linkages between the Ideals, Principles, and the Code as a whole.

Based on an activity by Cheryl Foster, Central Arizona College.

Activity 4.5: Is It Ethical? Game (Beginning)

In the Is It Ethical? Game, participants decide whether a fictional early childhood educator's response to a situation is *ethical* or *not ethical*. They then use the NAEYC Code of Ethical Conduct to assess their decision. Playing the game is fun and energizing, but can be time consuming, so you will want to plan accordingly. It is best played in groups of 4–6 and generally takes 30–45 minutes.

Preparation

- Make a set of game materials for each group of 4–6 players (see information on pages 109–119 in the Appendix). Each set should include Directions and Situation

Cards. Make each set on a different color of cardstock, and store each in a zip-top plastic bag so that the sets are sturdy and easy to reassemble for future use. There are two different sets of Situation Cards. Set A describes situations commonly encountered by practitioners who work directly with children, and Set B involves situations commonly encountered by program administrators.

- Make sure each player has a copy of the 2005/2011 edition of the NAEYC Code of Ethical Conduct (as well as the Supplement for Program Administrators, if you are using Set B) and a sheet of paper to tally their answers during play.

- The leader calls time. There are more situations in each set than your groups are likely to complete in a single session, and they will vary in how long it takes them to decide on, record, and discuss their responses. Do not call time until each participant has had a chance to read at least one Situation Card and their small group has reached its decision or agreed to disagree on its response to that situation.

- Participants will want to review the situations and know if they were "right." The leader will use the Answer Sheet to indicate if the response described on the card was **E** (ethical) or **NE** (not ethical) and identifies the Principle(s) and Ideals(s) that apply to each.

- The purpose of this game is to get participants to use the Code, but you can keep score if you want to. To keep score, players check their individual tally sheets as the leader labels each situation as **E** or **NE** and identifies the Principle(s) and Ideal(s) that apply. Players receive one point if they agreed with the Answer Sheet when voting **E** or **NE** and a second point if they found one or more of the matching Principles or Ideals from the list.

It is important for the leader to emphasize that everyone who plays the game is a winner, because all players benefit if they used the Code and made connections between their ethical choices and the Code's Principles and Ideals. The only way to lose is to fail to use the Code to help determine ethical responses. If you decide to score the game, add up points and congratulate the high scorers as well as everyone else.

Variation on Is It Ethical?

In this variation, individuals answer the question "Is it ethical?" as each Situation Card is read and records **E** or **NE** and the items in the Code that supports their decision on their tally sheet. When all members of the group have recorded their answers, they discuss them with each other. Then the dealer reads the answer from the Answer Sheet and identifies the items in the Code that support that answer. If players are keeping score, they receive one point if they agreed with the Answer Sheet when voting **E** or **NE** and a second point if they found one or more of the matching Principles or Ideals from the list.

Activity 4.6: Reflection on the NAEYC Code (Intermediate)

Have participants work with one or two partners to discuss the following reflection.

> *Reflection*: How did you first learn about the NAEYC Code of Ethical Conduct? What was your initial reaction to it? How have you used it in your work? In what ways have you found it helpful? (Feeney, Freeman, & Pizzolongo 2012, 20)

After the small groups have talked, reconvene the large group and discuss how the NAEYC Code has been helpful to them, how it might help them in the future, and how it can be helpful to others.

Activity 4.7: The Code and Me Panel Discussion (Advanced—this activity is suitable for a course or multi-session training)

Invite two or three experienced early childhood professionals with an interest in ethics to sit on a panel. Ask the members of the panel to respond to questions such as the following:

- How did you learn about the NAEYC Code of Ethical Conduct?
- How has the NAEYC Code of Ethical Conduct been helpful to you in addressing ethical responsibilities and dilemmas?
- How have you used the NAEYC Code of Ethical Conduct at different points in your career?
- What kinds of ethical issues and dilemmas come up regularly in your daily work?
- In your experience, what kinds of ethical responsibilities and dilemmas are most difficult to deal with for beginners? For more experienced practitioners? Why?
- Invite participants to pose their own questions to the panel (you might ask students to prepare some questions in advance and bring them to class).

Activity 4.8: Code/No Code Small Group Discussion (Advanced)

Divide participants into small groups. Select some of the cases found in the Selected Cases section of the Appendix (beginning on page 144) and distribute several to each of the groups.

Ask each group to discuss how a practitioner or program administrator would handle each situation without a code of ethics for guidance, compared to how each situation might be addressed with the help of the Code of Ethics.

After the groups have discussed the cases and considered how using a code of ethics might change an early childhood educator's actions, ask groups to discuss the following questions:

- Why do early childhood educators need a code of ethics?
- What happens when there is no code?
- How can having a code of ethics improve the quality of our work?
- How can having a code of ethics improve the status of the field of early childhood education?

Have a representative from each small group report back to the large group. Write the points that are made on chart paper or a whiteboard/blackboard and summarize the groups' conclusions.

Activity 4.9: Reflection on the Need for a Code of Ethics (Advanced)

Have participants work with one or two others to consider the following reflection about the need for a code of ethics.

Reflection: Do you think that these four aspects of working with young children (managing relationships with children, families, colleagues, and society) provide a strong case for the need for a code of ethics for the early childhood field? What experiences have you had with each one that supports your view? Are there other characteristics of the early childhood education field that suggest the need for a code of ethics? (Feeney, Freeman, & Pizzolongo 2012, 17)

Activity 4.10: Comparing Codes of Ethics (Advanced)

Divide participants into small groups and give each group a copy of NAEYC's Code of Ethical Conduct and Statement of Commitment, along with the code of ethics from another field. You can find the code of ethics of many organizations online (e.g., the Council for Exceptional Children [CEC], the National Association of Elementary School Principals [NAESP], the National Association of Social Workers [NASW], and North Carolina Public Schools). Ask participants to work together to find similarities and differences between the codes.

Reconvene the large group and have representatives from each small group report the similarities and differences they found in the codes. Discuss whether they noticed any unique characteristics of the NAEYC Code.

Variation on Comparing Codes of Ethics

Compare codes of ethics for early childhood educators from other nations (e.g., Australia, New Zealand, Singapore, Canada [British Columbia, Ontario, Nova Scotia]) with the NAEYC Code. Discuss why there are differences and what this suggests about practice in different places. You can find these codes by searching for them online.

Revision, Endorsement, and Enforcement

Information about how the Code is revised and NAEYC's efforts to promote its use and expand its reach are likely to be more meaningful to those who have some experience working with young children, and who have had a previous introduction to the Code.

You might want to point out that the Code is widely available and that some of the resources are easily available through NAEYC. In addition to the Code brochure, *Ethics and the Early Childhood Educator*, and this book, *Young Children*—NAEYC's highly respected, peer-reviewed journal—features a regular column, Focus on Ethics, that alternates with one column presenting a commonly occurring ethical dilemma followed by a column with that dilemma's analysis, informed by input from practitioners in the field.

Explain that the NAEYC Code of Ethical Conduct is not enforced because entrance into the field is not regulated (as is entrance into other recognized professions), and membership in NAEYC is open to all. Leaders in the field have taken the stance, nonetheless, that given the vulnerability of young children and the great disparity in power between children and their adult caregivers, even a voluntary code of ethics provides valuable safeguards for children in early care and education programs. If you are doing in-depth training or teaching several course sessions on ethics, you might want to explore the implications of code enforcement as it relates to early childhood education's efforts to achieve recognized professional status.

Activities concerned with the ramifications of code enforcement are most appropriate for learners who have had some experience with the Code and are interested in the professional status of the field of early childhood education.

Activity 4.11: Reflection on Code Enforcement (Advanced)

Have participants work in small groups of two or three to respond to the following reflection questions about Code enforcement.

Reflection: What would be the advantages of enforcing the NAEYC Code? What are the advantages of having it be voluntary? Which do you think is preferable and why? Do you think it is desirable to require everyone who works with young children to demonstrate knowledge of the Code and skill in applying it? (Feeney, Freeman, & Pizzolongo 2012, 22)

After small groups have talked, bring them together in the large group and discuss how an enforced code of ethics would differ from a voluntary code and the advantages and disadvantages of each.

Activity 4.12: Debate on Code Enforcement (Advanced)

This activity is useful with a group of confident and articulate participants who are interested in policy and would be comfortable with a formal debate structure. The activity should be planned ahead of time and will require 30–50 minutes.

What You Do

Select two small teams of debaters (two to three people in each group—larger teams make the debate confusing). Ask teams to prepare an argument either for or against the proposition that *the NAEYC Code of Ethical Conduct should be enforced.*

Give the team the following instructions for preparing for the debate:

- Construct a persuasive argument (several minutes in length) in support of your assigned position, explaining why enforcement is or is not a good idea.
- Anticipate the arguments of the opposing team. What sorts of arguments can they make in support of their position? Are there flaws with these arguments? How do they affect your case? How will you respond if they are brought up?
- Construct a rebuttal statement (several minutes in length) that critically analyzes the opposing team's argument based on what you anticipate they will say.

- Finally, make a third statement, a summation in which you pull together your strongest arguments and appeal to the audience. Give participants 1–2 minutes of preparation time between speeches.
- After the teams have presented their debates, point out the major issues that emerged.

Points to Emphasize in Your Teaching

- It is particularly important for early childhood educators to have a code of ethics because our actions can have a powerful impact on the very young children with whom we work.
- It is essential that learners understand the distinction between the Code's Ideals and Principles.
- Even though the Code is not enforced, it is widely disseminated and has a substantial impact on the field of early childhood education. It is included in professional standards, and many individuals and programs choose to follow it.
- The Code is like a roadmap that shows many ways to reach a destination—it rarely gives an easy answer to a dilemma. (Resolving dilemmas will be discussed in the chapter that follows.)

Five

Addressing Ethical Issues

An important function of the NAEYC Code is to provide early childhood educators with guidance for responding to the ethical issues they encounter in their work. This guidance is important because beginning educators often think that their personal morality will be sufficient to help them respond to the ethical challenges of the workplace. With experience, many find that their own morality does not provide enough guidance and they come to see the value of a code. That is why helping early childhood educators learn to address ethical issues effectively is one of the most important objectives for those who teach them professional ethics.

Note: Use the information in this chapter to teach participants about addressing ethical issues or, more specifically, to teach Chapter 3, "Addressing Ethical Issues," in *Ethics and the Early Childhood Educator*.

You may need to begin the process of teaching professional ethics by helping students understand that many of the problems they encounter in the workplace, or that they will encounter in their work in the future, have an ethical component. Once they understand that they are dealing with ethics, they may be more motivated to learn about the NAEYC Code and how it can help them handle the challenges they will invariably encounter during their careers.

Distinguishing Between Ethical Responsibilities and Ethical Dilemmas

After becoming acquainted with the Code, learners may be ready to analyze realistic ethical situations and to develop responses that answer the question "What should the ethical early childhood educator do?" To engage in this kind of analysis, they need to be able to identify the ethical responsibilities that are clearly spelled out in the Code and contrast them with ethical dilemmas. Ethical responsibilities are mandates—they describe what early childhood educators must or must not do. They describe how early childhood educators are required to act and are clearly spelled out in the Code.

(Ethical responsibilities are discussed on pages 24–25 of *Ethics and the Early Childhood Educator*.) Ethical dilemmas, on the other hand, involve conflicting responsibilities and have more than one possible resolution, each of which can be justified as being a viable choice. (Ethical dilemmas are discussed on pages 26–27 of *Ethics and the Early Childhood Educator*.) An ethical issue must be either a responsibility or a dilemma; it cannot be both.

The graphic below describes the essential first steps of resolving a workplace problem.

Addressing a Workplace Problem
Part I: Determine the Nature of the Problem

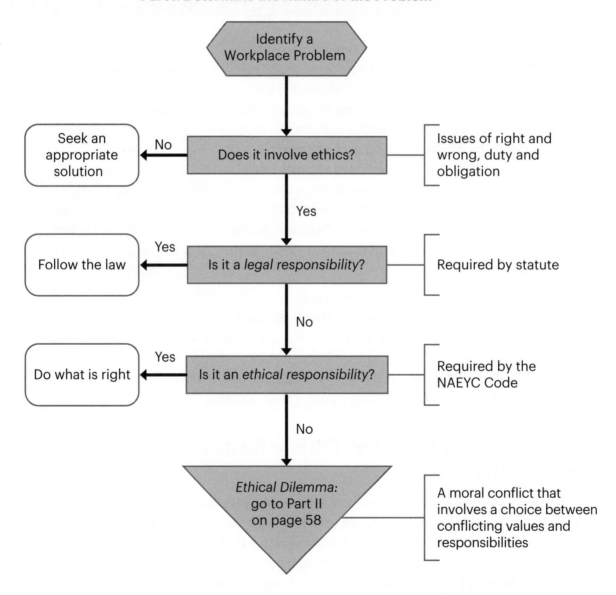

	Identify a Workplace Problem	
Seek an appropriate solution	← No — Does it involve ethics?	Issues of right and wrong, duty and obligation
Follow the law	← Yes — Is it a *legal responsibility*?	Required by statute
Do what is right	← Yes — Is it an *ethical responsibility*?	Required by the NAEYC Code
	Ethical Dilemma: go to Part II on page 58	A moral conflict that involves a choice between conflicting values and responsibilities

If the issue is actually a legal or ethical responsibility, the educator must follow the law or honor the responsibility. If the educator finds that the issue is indeed an ethical dilemma, then she or he needs to seek a resolution to the dilemma.

Helping students understand this distinction is essential if they are going to be equipped to appropriately address both kinds of situations. That means you must spend enough time learning about this distinction so the students with whom you work understand it too.

Activities About the Difference Between Ethical Responsibilities and Ethical Dilemmas

How to Identify Activities for Different Learners

Chapters 1, 3, 4, and 5 have activities that are designed to help students get to know each other and learn about and apply the NAEYC Code of Ethical Conduct. Each activity is identified as Icebreaker (Introductory), Beginning, Intermediate, or Advanced. The Icebreaker activities in Chapter 1 are designed to help participants get to know each other. Beginning activities are designed to promote understanding of basic concepts related to ethics and introduce the Code. Intermediate activities expand on basic knowledge of the Code. Advanced activities involve application and are for those who are acquainted with the Code and familiar with the process of ethical analysis.

Activity 5.1: Reflection About Ethical Responsibilities (Beginning)

Have participants think about and then write or discuss their responses to the following reflection about ethical responsibilities.

Reflection: Consider a situation that tempted you to do what was easy or popular or what others thought was correct rather than what you believed was right. What did you do? Were you able to keep sight of your responsibilities to children, families, and colleagues? How would you describe your thinking about it to someone new to the field? (Feeney, Freeman, & Pizzolongo 2012, 25)

Activity 5.2: What Kind of Issue Is It? (Intermediate)

This activity presents short descriptions of the kinds of issues early childhood educators are likely to encounter. Students work in groups to identify those that are *not* ethical *issues*, those that are *ethical responsibilities*, and those that are *ethical dilemmas*. This works well as an in-class activity for small groups of 2–5 and can be expected to take 30–45 minutes.

Preparation

- Make sure each participant has a copy of the NAEYC Code of Ethical Conduct.
- Make a set of game materials for each small group (2-5 participants). Materials and directions can be found on pages 120–136 (Activity 5.2) in the Appendix. Each set will include directions, 24 scenario cards, and three sorting sheets: one for situations that are not ethical issues, one for ethical responsibilities, and one for ethical dilemmas. (It would be helpful to copy each of these sorting sheets on different-colored paper.) Include Answer Sheets if you will have participants check their own answers.
- Make each set of scenario cards on a different color cardstock, and store each set of game materials in a zip-top plastic bag so that they are sturdy and easy to keep organized.
- Review the directions (in participants' sets of materials) to prepare them to complete the activity.
- The success students have sorting the cards correctly will indicate if they are able to identify issues that do not have an ethical component, and how well they understand the difference between ethical responsibilities and ethical dilemmas. It may help you know if they need additional support understanding these distinctions.

Activity 5.3: Is This an Ethical Responsibility or an Ethical Dilemma? (Intermediate)

This activity presents short descriptions of the kinds of issues early childhood educators are likely to encounter in their work. It asks participants to consider each and to identify which are *ethical responsibilities* (also referred to as *professional responsibilities*) and which are *ethical dilemmas*. They are also asked to identify items in the Code that would help them address this issue. This works well as an in-class activity for small groups of 2–5, or it can be a homework assignment for students to complete independently.

Preparation

- The materials for this activity can be found in the Appendix on pages 137–142 (Activity 5.3). Each set includes the directions, the definitions of ethical responsibilities and ethical dilemmas, and five short scenarios.

- Make sure each participant has a copy of the NAEYC Code of Ethical Conduct (2005/2011).
- Review the directions to prepare participants to complete the activity.
- If this is an in-class activity, the presenter can refer to the Answer Sheets to lead participants in evaluating their answers, or can include the Answer Sheets with the other materials so that small groups can check their work after they have considered each of the scenarios.

A Framework for Addressing Ethical Issues

Once you are sure that participants are able to distinguish between ethical responsibilities and ethical dilemmas, you can focus on helping them learn how to analyze situations that involve ethics and use items from the Code, in combination with informed professional judgment, to find resolutions to dilemmas. Developing skill in analyzing realistic cases is essential because no code can anticipate every situation or provide guidance for every ethical issue that early childhood educators will encounter in the workplace. From the beginning of its work on professional ethics in the l980s, NAEYC has solicited information about the real-life ethical issues that members are facing and used these situations as the basis for developing and revising the Code. The cases have been used extensively as training resources in workshops and courses.

Early childhood education is in step with many other professions that use case analysis to teach professional ethics. Our experience is like that of Elizabeth Campbell, who wrote: "I have found that the students enjoy case study analysis, and the more deeply they engage with the language of ethical principles, the more likely they are to discover the layers of moral and ethical complexity that they may have overlooked at first" (Campbell 2013, 40).

No matter what their level of experience, it is helpful to provide a framework that guides educators in applying professional guidelines to examining realistic scenarios (Brophy-Herb, Kostelnik, & Stein 2001; Feeney, Freeman, & Pizzolongo 2012; Johnson, Vare, & Evers 2013; Warnick & Silverman 2011).

The graphic on the following page summarizes the framework for analyzing an ethical dilemma, which is further elaborated below.

1. **Identify the conflicting responsibilities.** To whom do you have responsibilities in this situation (children, families, colleagues, the community and society) and what do you owe to each one?
2. **Brainstorm possible resolutions.** List all of the possible ways that you might be able to resolve this dilemma.

Part II: Analyze the Dilemma

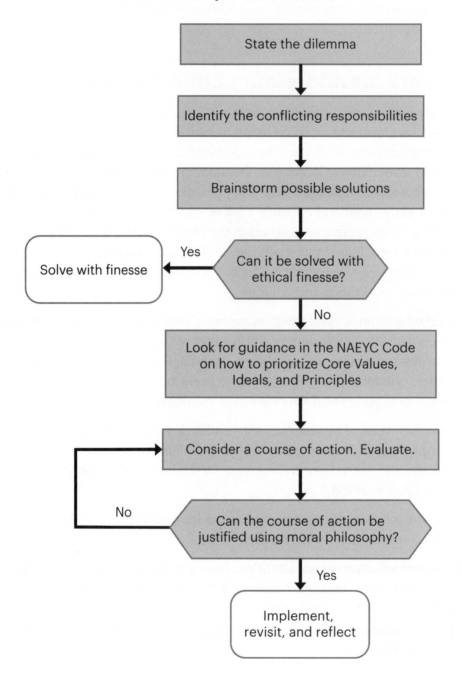

State the dilemma

↓

Identify the conflicting responsibilities

↓

Brainstorm possible solutions

↓

Can it be solved with ethical finesse? — Yes → Solve with finesse

No ↓

Look for guidance in the NAEYC Code on how to prioritize Core Values, Ideals, and Principles

↓

Consider a course of action. Evaluate.

↓

Can the course of action be justified using moral philosophy? — No → (back to Consider a course of action)

Yes ↓

Implement, revisit, and reflect

3. **Consider ethical finesse.** Think about a way to resolve the problem that would be satisfactory to everyone involved and that would avoid having to make a difficult decision. Then assume that you have tried ethical finesse and it has not been effective, so you need to move on to the next step of finding a justifiable resolution.

4. **Look for guidance in the NAEYC Code.** Carefully review the Core Values, Ideals, and Principles in the Code that relate to this situation. List the relevant items and identify how they apply.

5. **Decide on a justifiable course of action.** Select what you think is the most ethically justifiable resolution to your dilemma. This resolution will combine guidance from the Code with your best professional judgment. It should be consistent with your values and those of the early childhood field. Discuss how you applied items from the Code and how you prioritized them.

If you use cases in your course or workshop, begin with those included in this book, those in *Ethics and the Early Childhood Educator*, and cases that have been included in the Focus on Ethics columns in *Young Children* (search "Focus on Ethics" on the NAEYC website). It is a good idea to begin with these sources, because developing scenarios that are actual dilemmas is more difficult than it might seem. Keep in mind that a productive discussion about an ethical dilemma requires at least 45 minutes.

When you include case analysis in your courses, it is a good idea to structure small groups to ensure that every student's opinions will be heard and respectfully considered. It is also helpful to arrange groups so that they are heterogeneous. That will increase the chances that participants will hear various perspectives. Another suggestion is to change the composition of groups from one class session to the next, so students don't just talk to like-minded friends who are not likely to stretch their thinking.

The opportunity to discuss ethics cases with peers gives learners opportunities to

- Be part of a community of learners
- Listen to the viewpoints of others
- Think through a situation and articulate and support a position
- Deal with ambiguity and increase their understanding of a range of viewpoints
- Learn to challenge the thinking of others and respond to challenges
- Articulate arguments that move from immediate action to ethical principles

Described below are several strategies to support learners in addressing dilemmas, beginning with activities that are appropriate for beginners and progressing to more challenging activities that are appropriate for advanced practitioners. Beginners are just becoming aware that ethical issues occur frequently in early childhood settings and are learning that the NAEYC Code is a useful tool for addressing them. Use the framework described above to introduce them to the Code and get them started using it to address ethical issues. The first step is to determine the nature of the problem. Does it involve ethics? If so, is it a dilemma or a responsibility? Learners ready to take the next step should identify the early childhood educator's responsibilities or identify the stakeholders in the dilemma. It is usually enough to help beginners practice these first steps in the process and gain some familiarity with the kinds of ethical issues early childhood educators are likely to encounter in their work.

If you have enough time with beginners, or if you are working with slightly more advanced learners, you can guide them through the entire case analysis process, from identifying a problem, determining if it is an ethical issue, deciding if it is a responsibility or dilemma, considering ethical finesse, and finally deciding on an ethically defensible course of action.

Activities to Teach About Resolving Ethical Dilemmas

Activity 5.4: Reflection About Experience With Dilemmas (Intermediate)

Have participants think of and then write about or discuss their experience with a dilemma—a situation that involves two justifiable resolutions.

Reflection: Have you ever been in a situation in which you had to choose between two alternatives that both could be justified? What were the competing interests? How did you respond? How did you think through what was the right thing to do? (Feeney, Freeman, & Pizzolongo 2012, 29)

Activity 5.5: Reflection on Hard Decisions (Intermediate)

Have participants think of and then write about or discuss a situation that required them to make a hard ethical decision.

Reflection: Think about a time when you made a hard decision as you addressed an ethical dilemma. Who were the stakeholders, and what were your obligations to each? What resources did you use to help you resolve the dilemma? What was the outcome? Was it successful? (Feeney, Freeman, & Pizzolongo 2012, 33)

Activity 5.6: Analyzing an Ethical Dilemma (Intermediate)

Use the case analysis framework on pages 54 and 58 of this chapter to analyze a dilemma—either one found in an NAEYC-published resource or one that participants in your training have experienced in their work. As they analyze the dilemma, be sure that students follow the framework to ensure that all of the steps are addressed in the right order.

Participants who have had a great deal of experience working with young children and families and are adept at debriefing ethical dilemmas may be ready to develop a dilemma of their own. For example, graduate students might describe and analyze dilemmas that they have encountered in their workplaces as a capstone assignment for a master's course or program. Activity 5.7 includes guidelines that students might find helpful when writing about dilemmas they have experienced. However, even mature, experienced, and able students may need a great deal of support identifying and describing a dilemma.

Activity 5.7: Writing an Ethical Dilemma (Advanced)

Tell participants to write their dilemmas as an engaging story. (You might want to limit the scenarios to 500 words to encourage students to write precisely and to polish their work carefully.)

The dilemma needs to be a situation for which there is more than one possible resolution, each of which can be morally justified. Participants need to identify all of the stakeholders to whom they have responsibilities and what their responsibility is to each one. Each scenario should lead them to ask, "What should the ethical early childhood educator do? Should she or he do this or do that?"

Activity 5.8: My Dilemma (Advanced)

Note: This activity works well in a short course or half-day workshop with experienced practitioners who have worked with cases in another activity.

_____

Participants should already have had experience thinking about the differences between dilemmas and responsibilities. This activity is designed to help them realize that the Code of Ethical Conduct has practical applications for their day-to-day work and to build a disposition to use it. Participants work in small groups.

What to Do

- Have participants form an even number of small groups. Distribute index cards of two different colors to the groups, giving half one color and half the other color. Ask participants (as individuals) to write (anonymously) an ethical situation from their own professional lives on a card. Ask them to finish each scenario with a question that describes two possible actions (e.g., "Do you refuse the parent's request and allow the child to play in the sandbox, or do you find another activity for the child?").

- When participants are done writing, collect the cards for each group and redistribute to a different group, making sure that each receives a different color card than the one they wrote on.

- In small groups,

  » One group member reads a scenario aloud.

  » The group decides whether or not it is, in fact, an ethical dilemma. If it isn't, is it an ethical responsibility or simply an issue of professional practice (a scenario that does not have an ethical component)?

  » Individuals search the Code to identify the Core Values, Ideals, and Principles involved, then come together to share their findings and agree—if it is an ethical responsibility, what is the ethical course of action? If it is a dilemma, has the person correctly identified the possible ethical responses—if not, what are they?

  » Continue with additional scenarios until time is called.

- In the large group,

  » Each small group selects one item they agreed was a dilemma and shares their resolutions.

  » The large group discusses each group's conclusions, using the Code as a resource.

  » The participants whose dilemma was chosen is invited, if they so desire, to add additional information or share how they handled the dilemma. They may also choose to remain anonymous.

Activity 5.9: Children's Literature Connections (Intermediate)

The following children's books are good starting points for discussing ethical issues:

- *Nasreddine,* by Odile Weulersse, illustrates the idea that you cannot please everyone when making a moral decision, and that individuals must do what they think is right.
- *Hey, Little Ant,* by Phillip and Hannah Hoose, provides a lesson about making choices and the value of a life.

Providing More Challenge for Experienced Educators

When you work with experienced educators whose understanding of the ethical dimensions of their practice is well developed, you can help them to understand the nuances of ethical decision making and support them in developing higher levels of ethical reasoning. You do this by providing opportunities for them to discuss ethical issues with each other and by asking them questions designed to challenge their thinking. Good questions engage learners in ways that can advance their stage of moral development.

Experienced educators might also be ready to learn about theories of moral philosophy that can inform ethical decision making. The first ethical theory, utilitarianism, looks at the consequences of an action and seeks the greatest good for the greatest number of people. The second considers the rightness or wrongness of an act rather than its consequences. It asks, "What if everyone acted this way?" The third philosophical approach, referred to as the ethic of care, is sometimes expressed as the Golden Rule, "Do unto others as you would have others do unto you." After they have gone through the process of analyzing a dilemma, have your students consider how these theories can give them insight into the implications of a proposed resolution.

Some advanced students may be interested in the philosophic underpinnings for the items in the NAEYC Code. You could introduce them to some widely embraced ethical principles, such as

- **Respect for autonomy:** Enabling individuals to make reasoned and informed choices when they are capable of doing so
- **Beneficence:** Acting in the best interests of the person served
- **Nonmaleficence:** Not causing harm (the basis for P-1.1 in the NAEYC Code)
- **Justice:** Equal and fair distribution of resources
- **Fidelity:** Loyalty, fairness, truthfulness, honoring commitments and keeping promises, and dedication to those served

Supporting the Development of Moral Reasoning

Teaching professional ethics involves more than helping individuals learn about morality and ethics and the NAEYC Code of Ethical Conduct. Another important purpose for ethics instruction is to help learners develop higher levels of moral reasoning (the ability to understand moral concepts and to engage in increasingly higher levels of moral reflection).

Darlene Daneker (2007) points out that in order to understand a code of ethics and use it to deal with the complex ethical demands of the workplace, professionals need to have reached a stage of moral development that enables them to understand and apply the principles in a code of ethics. The fact that an individual's stage of moral development is connected to their ability to use a code of ethics productively makes it clear how important it is to help learners increase their moral reasoning abilities. Lawrence Kohlberg's and Carol Gilligan's theories of moral development (discussed in Chapter 2) describe the course of moral development and suggest that students can attain higher levels when they have opportunities to engage in focused discussions about ethical issues.

Researchers in counseling, dentistry, and other fields (Bebeau 1993, 1994; Daneker 2007) have documented how the systematic study of professional ethics can have a positive impact on students' ability to do moral reasoning. Their research has demonstrated that the best way to support this growth is to use teaching methods that involve structured case analysis and focused discussions of ethical issues. They have found that giving students opportunities to discuss ethical issues with peers, particularly those whose level of ethical reasoning is just a bit more advanced than their own, can help learners to increase their appreciation for the complexity of ethical issues and to reach more mature levels of thinking.

If you wish to go beyond the basics in your teaching of professional ethics, you can provide learners with opportunities to increase their skill in moral reasoning through having them engage in in-depth analysis of ethical dilemmas, coupled with teaching strategies that expand and challenge their thinking.

Helping Learners Examine Assumptions and Expand Their Thinking

When you understand that the responses to moral situations that you hear from learners is a function of their stage of moral development, you will be better able to support them in thinking more deeply. It is possible to help students examine their assumptions and think about alternatives in ways that will help them achieve a higher level of moral reasoning. This process takes time and requires skill.

An important part of your role as a teacher of professional ethics is to ask questions that expand learners' frame of reference and create dissonance between what *is* and what *could be* in the ethical cases examined. Asking the kinds of probing questions listed below can help learners develop and hone their skills in moral reasoning.

1. Why do you think that rule/practice was created—what is the reason for it?
2. Is there another way to think about that?
3. How could we change that rule/practice to honor the other person's/group's needs?
4. Is it always the correct thing to do? Why?
5. What might a person with a different point of view say about that?
6. Is there a way to meet both groups'/people's needs?
7. What would you gain/lose if you did it the other person's/group's way?
8. What decision results in the greatest good for the majority while honoring the minority (and vice versa)?
9. What is the immediate impact of that decision? What might be the long-term impact?
10. What is the kindest thing you could do in this situation? Why?
11. What's the hardest thing to do in this situation? Why?
12. What would be the bravest thing to do in this situation? Why?
13. Imagine that you are the other person (parent, teacher, director, licensing worker, etc.). What would you tell me about the situation? Why?
14. How could you let the _____ (parent, teacher, director, licensing worker, etc.) know you understand his or her needs/perspective?
15. What would happen if there were no rule about this?
16. What would be the consequence of doing nothing?
17. If the story of this situation appeared in the local paper, would you be ashamed or proud to see your name/your group's name and action publicized? Why?
18. What do you think someone you respected (parent, minister, rabbi, mentor) would say was right in this situation? Why?

Barriers to Systematic Analysis of Ethical Dilemmas

How learners approach ethical issues may stand in their way of systematic decision making. First, many individuals expect to find the correct answer to the dilemmas they encounter clearly spelled out in the Code. It takes some effort to help them understand that there is rarely (if ever) an easy resolution to an ethical dilemma. They also need to understand that the more complex and difficult the dilemma is, the more likely it is that it will require a good deal of professional judgment to supplement the guidance provided by the Code.

Second, beginners tend to rely on their first intuitive response to a situation and often find it unfamiliar and uncomfortable to work through dilemmas slowly and deliberately. Requiring them to work through the dilemma using the process described above slows them down and makes it more likely they will turn to the Code rather than rely only on their instincts. In response to a discussion in an ethics workshop we presented, Cynthia Paris, associate professor and director of the laboratory school at the University of Delaware, wrote to us, "Whatever ethical action is taken, it should be done with patience and persistence and ongoing examination and willingness to change to a different ethical path if necessary. I've found it challenging helping young teachers get past looking for the *one* quick response that will take care of it, that I believe persistence and patience are required of a professional." (quoted with permission)

Finally, as mentioned in Chapter 2, early childhood educators tend to be kind and nurturing people and are reluctant to reach a decision that might make another person unhappy. Yet it is in the nature of many ethical issues that the needs and interests of one stakeholder must take precedence over those of another. Participants may arrive first at a resolution designed to please everyone involved in a dilemma. It may be hard for them to think about what to do if it doesn't work the way they think it should. When early childhood ethics workshops were first conducted, University of Hawaii philosophy professor Kenneth Kipnis would challenge participants who were deliberating about a dilemma by saying, "Okay, let's say you tried that, and it didn't work. What will you do next?" He did this until every alternative for addressing the problem without displeasing someone had been tried and failed. After every option had been exhausted, participants were ready to make a hard decision. (See the nap case on pages 59–63 of *Ethics and the Early Childhood Educator* as an example of how a teacher can work through this process.) Use this approach to help participants find the courage to make the difficult decisions that are sometimes called for when dealing with dilemmas.

How to Handle Saying No

Learners may think that once they have decided on a resolution to a dilemma, the situation is over. But it is not. The fact that every ethical dilemma has two defensible resolutions means that early childhood educators, whose nature may be to want to please everyone and get along, must sometimes go against a friend's, a colleague's, or a parent's wishes and say no. They need to communicate this difficult decision diplomatically, a task that is particularly challenging when they have to inform the person who isn't going to get what they wanted. An important part of helping students learn to address ethical dilemmas is to help them think about how to preserve relationships by communicating their decision in a kind, respectful, and supportive way.

Here are some things you can say to preserve and honor relationships when you communicate a difficult decision:

1. You and I disagree. I believe (the proposed action) would be harmful to the (children/ child/families/family) so I cannot (agree to/support) it. Let's think of something else (we/you) could do instead.

2. You believe (the proposed action) is desirable for the (children/child/families/family). But I feel that to do so would be (negative, nonsupportive, harmful). Feeling this way, it would be unethical for me to (participate/agree). Would you work with me to come up with another plan?

3. I know you feel (the proposed action) would be fair to the (children/child/families/ family); however, I feel that to do so would be discriminatory. So it wouldn't be right. Let's see if we can think of an alternative.

4. It would be (easier/less complicated) to make this decision without involving everyone. But it is important for everyone concerned to have a voice, and it's what the Code of Ethical Conduct tells us we should do. Let's think of the best way to involve them.

5. I know you feel that you have done all you can. However, I believe we can still (build relationships/make adaptations/consult), so it would be premature to remove the child at this time. When we have tried some additional strategies, if we still are not able to meet the child's needs or if the child is jeopardizing other children, we can work with the child's family and specialists to determine the next steps.

6. Because we have reasonable cause to suspect (child abuse/neglect), we have a legal and ethical responsibility to report it. I cannot agree to wait and see if things will get better. We can inform the family that the referral (will be/has been) made.

7. I realize it would be (easier/less disruptive) to not do (the proposed action). However, it's what the Code of Ethical Conduct tells us we should do. So let's think of the best way to do (the proposed action).

8. I know you would like us to support your (court petition/custody request). However, the Code of Ethical Conduct for our field directs us to refrain from being an advocate when family members are in conflict. So we are not able to say that we think you should have custody. We can, however, share our observations of your child. My observations may help the (judge/mediator) make an informed decision.

9. I realize your coworker's (sex/race/national origin/religious beliefs/affiliation/age/ marital status/family structure/disability/sexual orientation) is uncomfortable for you. However, I believe your (suggestion/request) to do (the proposed action) would be discriminatory, and I can't discriminate against or condone discrimination against a coworker.

10. I understand you have concerns about (coworker's) behavior. But unless it involves potential harm to (a child/children), I can't discuss it because our Code of Ethical Conduct directs you to first let (him/her) know of your concern and attempt to resolve it collegially and confidentially. Please do this first.

11. Even though neither of us agrees with this policy, I believe we need to follow it and attempt to change it constructively. Let's think of some ways we might get (the organization/administration) to change the policy.

Activity 5.10: Communicating the Resolution of a Dilemma (Intermediate)

Have learners review the list of things to say to preserve relationships, and then look at scenario 2.1 on page 145 of the Appendix. It concerns a 4-year-old child whose mother asks that he not be allowed to nap at school, but his teacher believes he needs to nap to have a good afternoon. Have them practice with a partner how they would tell the child's mother that, at least at the present time, they are going to have to decline her request and will let him nap at school. Have students work in pairs to develop, and then share, their best attempt to communicate with the mother in a respectful and supportive way. Have the large group consider which were the most effective strategies for communicating this difficult decision. This activity can be repeated with other dilemmas described in the Appendix of this book or in the Focus on Ethics column in *Young Children*, or with other dilemmas that students are particularly interested in.

Increase Ethical Commitment

Your observations of students' performance in class and evaluations of their written work give you opportunities to assess their knowledge of professional ethics and their skill in applying the NAEYC Code to hypothetical scenarios. But the real goal of professional ethics instruction is to increase students' ethical behavior—that is, their commitment to applying what they have learned in the workplace. In the end it is how they interact with children, families, colleagues, and supervisors that is the real measure of our success. Are they committed to pursuing what is just, right, and fair? Do they have the courage to take a principled position when they could choose an easier or more popular path? Will the ideals and principles they have learned about actually guide their day-to-day professional conduct?

Our Hope

We hear from both beginning and advanced students that studying ethics has had a lasting impact on their behavior at work, but the truth is that success is difficult to measure. We remain hopeful, however, that knowledge about the Code and reliance on it is increasing, and that we will see undeniable evidence that teaching about ethics has, in fact, resulted in an early childhood workforce that holds itself up to high ethical principles. It is our hope that all teachers of young children bring ethical knowledge, dispositions, and skills to the classroom every day, and that these qualities will be reflected in everything teachers do.

Consider the Following

It will promote constructive ethical deliberation if you can, to the greatest extent possible, structure heterogeneous groups and help participants learn to listen to each other and agree and disagree respectfully.

Good questions promote higher levels of moral reasoning. Practice asking challenging questions and allow enough time for students to construct thoughtful responses.

To engage in ethical deliberation, learners must be able to differentiate ethical issues from other kinds of issues.

To engage in ethical deliberation, learners must understand the difference between ethical responsibilities and ethical dilemmas.

Points to Emphasize in Your Teaching

- Ethical situations are often messy. They have been described as "ill-structured events," that have "no clear specified goal, usually incomplete information, and multiple solution paths" (Keefer et al. 2014, 250).
- There are no quick resolutions to resolving ethical dilemmas. They require slow and thoughtful deliberation.
- The more complex and difficult the dilemma is, the more it requires professional judgment in addition to guidance from the Code to reach a justifiable resolution.
- The first, intuitive response to resolving a dilemma is rarely adequate.
- Early childhood educators need to have the courage to come to decisions that do not please everyone involved in a situation.
- Working through well-constructed cases is an effective strategy for helping educators learn to address ethical dilemmas.
- The resolution to an ethical dilemma needs to be communicated in a way that honors and preserves relationships.

Six

Putting the Pieces Together

This chapter includes brief descriptions of how ethics instruction can be organized for different groups of learners in a variety of settings. It describes several instructional formats, from one-hour training sessions to semester-long projects that engage students in the in-depth analysis of ethical issues. It also presents an example of an assignment for undergraduates that is designed as a continuing thread throughout an advanced practicum or student teaching seminar, and another that is an appropriate capstone assignment for a graduate program. These examples are intended give you some ideas about how to put the pieces of an ethics training together for different settings and to meet the needs of college students, teachers, and administrators at different stages of their professional development.

Components of Training Sessions

What follows is a brief description of recommended components to include in most ethics training sessions. The depth of the coverage of these topics depends on the length of the training, and the learners' previous experiences and their needs. Be sure to begin with an enthusiastic welcome for everyone. Start each session the same way, and then introduce additional elements based on the nature of the group, the setting, and the purpose of the training.

- **Welcome/Introduction**
  - » Who am I? Why me? Establish your experience/expertise.
  - » Who are you? What is your role? (show of hands)
    - Classroom teacher
    - Administrator of a program for children
    - Two-year college faculty member
    - Four-year college faculty member
    - Organization that provides professional development, such as a resource and referral program or agency
    - Other

» What do you know about the Code? (show of hands)
  – Have you heard of the NAEYC Code of Ethical Conduct?
  – Have you read the Code?
  – Have you used the Code to address ethical issues in your work?
  – Have you taught others about the Code and its application?

■ **Purpose and objectives of the session.** Some are described on page 5 of Chapter 1.

■ **Ground rules and why they are important.** More information is on page 8 of Chapter 1.

■ **Orientation.** It is best to begin a course or workshop with an orientation that can be called Ethics 101. Use this opportunity to introduce or review the definitions of *ethics* and *morality* and other related terms that are included in the Code (and are also in the glossary of this book). Even experienced educators who are familiar with professional ethics appreciate having this review that gets everyone on the same page.

■ **The role of ethics in a profession.** Begin a course or workshop by pointing out that all professions have codes of professional ethics that spell out professionals' responsibilities and offer them guidelines for resolving ethical dilemmas they encounter in the workplace. A code also describes to the public how they can count on the profession's members to behave. If you are teaching beginners, briefly touch on the role that codes of ethics play in professions. With experienced educators, you can explore the topic in more depth. It is essential to emphasize how important it is that early childhood educators understand their moral commitments because they have the potential to have such a powerful impact on the lives of children and families.

■ **Personal values and personal morality.** Stress that personal values and personal morality are a prerequisite to, but are not sufficient for, dealing with ethical issues in the early childhood workplace. The Wall of Personal Values, Activity 3.6 on page 28 of Chapter 3, is a good way to help make this distinction.

■ **Professional ethics and codes of ethics.** Explain that professions have distinctive values and ethical commitments that are expressed in their codes of ethics. You might ask participants to reflect on "Why is it important for a profession to have a code of ethics?"

■ **The NAEYC Code of Ethical Conduct.** After a general discussion of the role of a code of ethics in a profession, mention that early childhood education has a widely disseminated Code, and move to a discussion of the NAEYC Code. Describe its sections, which identify our responsibilities to children, families, colleagues, and community: Preamble, Core Values, and Ideals and Principles. Depending on the audience, you might also mention the Supplements for Adult Educators (NAEYC, NAECTE, & ACCESS 2004) and/or Program Administrators (NAEYC 2006).

- **Addressing ethical issues.** After you have laid this foundation, address the knowledge and skills from the list below that are most appropriate for your particular group of trainees. These are the essential elements of ethical competence learners need to master if they are to become adept at addressing ethical issues in the workplace.
  - » Recognizing the difference between ethical issues and other kinds of issues.
  - » Recognizing the difference between ethical responsibilities and ethical dilemmas.
  - » Learning to use a case analysis framework, such as the one in Chapter 5, on pages 57–60, to guide the analysis of situations with ethical dimensions.
  - » Developing strategies for respectfully declining a request when it has been decided that refusing is the most ethical response.
  - » Applying the three philosophic approaches to thinking about resolutions to ethical dilemmas, as outlined in Chapter 2, pages 21–22, and explained further on pages 31–32 in *Ethics and the Early Childhood Educator*. (This is appropriate for advanced students.)
  - » Developing skill in ethical reasoning. Strategies for supporting this skill are presented in Chapter 5.
  - » Writing an ethical dilemma.
- **Closing words/questions.** End a session by thanking participants for their interest, contributions, and commitment to the well-being of children and families, and ask if they have any questions. You might read a children's book, such as *The Empty Pot*, that puts the focus on morality and ethical decision making. If appropriate, share your contact information with the group.

Formats for Training

The sections that follow describe some of the typical contexts in which professional ethics in early childhood education are taught, and they suggest some ways that the content can be organized.

Basic Introduction in a Workshop, In-Service Session, or College Class

The intended audience for this introduction to professional ethics is beginning preservice teachers and teachers who are fairly new to the field of early childhood education.

The purpose of this kind of session is to help learners develop an awareness of the ethical responsibilities of teachers of young children, and to introduce them to the NAEYC Code. The intent is to involve participants, to help them understand that a code of ethics is an important aspect of every profession, to make them aware that early childhood educators regularly face ethical issues in their work, and to help them appreciate that the NAEYC Code of Ethical Conduct is a resource they can turn to when they encounter one of these ethical issues in their work.

The content of an introductory session will vary slightly based on the experience of the participants. In a college class, students may not have had experience working with young children or prior knowledge of the field's professional ethics. In an in-service or conference session, participants may have more real-world experience to share and may know that a code of ethics exists for early childhood educators.

Duration: 1–2 hours

Session outline

- Welcome/Introduction
- Purpose and objectives of the workshop
- Introductory activity (if time allows; see Chapter 1 for some options)
- Orientation
  - » Explain definitions.
  - » Identify the role of ethics in a profession.
  - » Identify participants' personal values.
  - » Differentiate personal values and morality and ethics from professional values and ethics.
  - » Read a picture book that illustrates personal morality (e.g., *The Empty Pot*) or the difference between values and preferences (e.g., *Bread and Jam for Frances*).
- Introduction to the NAEYC Code of Ethical Conduct
  - » Identify the Code's Core Values.
  - » Review the Code's four sections that describe our ethical responsibilities to children, families, colleagues, and community and society.
  - » Point out the Ideals and Principles in each section of the Code, and explain how Ideals and Principles are different from each other.
- Activity 4.5: Is It Ethical? (see Chapter 4, page 46). This game helps learners appreciate how the Code can help early childhood educators address commonly occurring situations that involve ethics.
- Closing words/questions

Follow-Up Session for Beginners

The intended audience for this follow-up or slightly more advanced session is individuals who have participated in the basic introduction session and college students and teachers who have already had some introduction to the Code and its contributions to the field.

The purpose of this session is for learners to appreciate the contributions the Code can make to their work with young children and families, and to become acquainted with the process they can use for resolving ethical dilemmas.

Duration: 2–3 hours

Session outline

- Begin in the same way as the introductory session above, unless this session occurs immediately after learners' basic introduction to ethics.
- Address the difference between ethical responsibilities and ethical dilemmas.
  - » Do Activity 5.2: What Kind of Issue Is It? (see Chapter 5, page 56).
  - » Read a picture book, such as *Hey, Little Ant*, that illustrates a situation that requires ethical deliberation.
- Introduce the case analysis framework (see pages 57–60).
- Choose a case from the collection in the Appendix or another case found in NAEYC's publications. Have participants work in small groups to use the case analysis framework to guide them in reaching a defensible resolution. Plan for this case analysis to take at least 45 minutes.
  - » Have small groups describe their resolution to the dilemma to the large group.
  - » If there is time, ask all participants to reflect on their experience working through this deliberate process to find a resolution to the kind of dilemma they are likely to encounter in their work.
  - » Provide time for closing words and questions.

Workshop for Program Administrators

The intended audience for this workshop is directors of early childhood programs. Participants are probably experienced educators who are aware of the NAEYC Code of Ethical Conduct, but they may not know that there is a Supplement for Program Administrators designed to help them address the unique ethical dimensions of their work.

The purpose of this session is to provide a brief refresher or introduction to the NAEYC Code, and for participants to become acquainted with the Supplement for Program Administrators. The session is designed to help them to understand that, when used as a companion to the Code, the Supplement can help participants address the kinds of ethical issues they frequently encounter.

Duration: 3 hours

Session outline

- Welcome/Introduction
- Orientation
  - » Explain definitions.
  - » Contrast professional ethics and personal morality.
    - Read a picture book that illustrates personal morality, such as *The Empty Pot*.
  - » Discuss why a code of ethics is important.
    - Individual Reflection: Do Activity 4.9: Reflection on the Need for a Code of Ethics (see Chapter 4, page 49).

- Individuals share their reflections with a partner, then with the group.
- Discuss the importance of having a code of ethics for early childhood educators (see page 13 in *Ethics and the Early Childhood Educator*).

- Brief introduction to the NAEYC Code of Ethical Conduct
  » Identify the Code's Core Values.
  » Review the Code's four sections that describe our ethical responsibilities to children, families, colleagues, and community and society.
  » Point out the Ideals and Principles in each section of the Code, and explain how Ideals and Principles are different from each other.
- Introduction to the Supplement for Program Administrators
  » Predict: "What might be its additional Core Values?"
  » Predict: "What might be its additional Ideals and Principles?"
  » Review the Supplement.
  » Explain that the Supplement does not stand alone—it is designed to be used in conjunction with the Code.
- Addressing ethical dilemmas
  » Define an ethical dilemma.
  » Define/give examples of ethical finesse.
  » Play the administrator version of Activity 4.5: Is It Ethical? Game (see Chapter 4, page 46).
  » Provide time for closing words and questions.

Advanced Practicum or Student Teaching Seminar

The intended audience for this assignment is preservice teachers enrolled in an advanced practicum or student teaching seminar. The students need to be spending several hours each week working with children in an early childhood program. This experience will work best if they are all in the same setting, and the director at the practicum site is familiar with the NAEYC Code.

The assignment involves students working together in a group to learn to recognize a real-life ethical issue that a member of the class has encountered in her or his work with children and families, to differentiate ethical responsibilities from ethical dilemmas, and to practice identifying a justifiable resolution to the real-life issue. This assignment can be used as a Key Assessment to address Standard 6b of NAEYC Standards for Early Childhood Professional Preparation: "Knowing about and upholding ethical standards and other professional guidelines." A rubric evaluating students' understanding can be found in Chapter 7 on pages 87–88.

Objectives

The objectives for this assignment are for students to

- Learn about the NAEYC Code of Ethical Conduct

- Demonstrate their ability to identify ethical issues and to differentiate ethical responsibilities from ethical dilemmas
- Demonstrate their ability to use the Code to resolve an ethical issue in the workplace
- Demonstrate their ability to summarize the process of ethical decision making and reflect on the contribution the NAEYC Code of Ethical Conduct can make to the work of early childhood educators

The sequence of instruction

Total duration: 2–3 hours, spread out over an entire term

Distribute copies of the Code of Ethical Conduct with course materials at the beginning of the term.

Part 1—Introductory session

Duration: 30 minutes to 1 hour

- Ask students to share what they remember about the Code from their earlier coursework.
  - » Review the four sections of the Code, and the Principles and Ideals in each.
  - » If students need to refresh their memories, do the Ethical Code Puzzle (Activity 4.3 in Chapter 4, page 45) or the Is It Ethical? Game (Activity 4.5 in Chapter 4, page 46).
- Review the definitions of responsibilities and dilemmas.
  - » If students need to refresh their memories, do What Kind of Issue Is It? (Activity 5.2 in Chapter 5, page 56) or Is This an Ethical Responsibility or an Ethical Dilemma? (Activity 5.3 in Chapter 5, page 56).
- Explain that the students are to be alert to any ethical issues they encounter while working with children and families in their practicum/student teaching site this term, and they should be prepared to describe and discuss any issue that arises at the next class meeting.

Part 2—When an ethical issue occurs

Duration: 30 minutes to one hour, during a practicum seminar when an ethical issue has arisen

- When a possible ethical issue arises, a student describes it to the group.
- The group discusses the issue and determines if it is an ethical issue. If it is ethical, they proceed to the analysis described below; if it does not involve ethics, the group tables that issue and postpones this activity until an ethical issue is brought forward for discussion.
- The group uses relevant sections of the Code to identify the stakeholders in the ethical issue being discussed.
- The group uses the Code to determine if it is an ethical responsibility or an ethical dilemma.

- Using the Code and other resources, class members identify a range of ethically defensible courses of action, including ethical finesse.
- A course of action is agreed upon and implemented (if doing so is possible in the practicum/student teaching setting).

Part 3—Students reflect on the process

- Students write a one-page report describing the situation, identifying it as being either an ethical responsibility or an ethical dilemma. If it was a dilemma, they identify the conflicting ethical responsibilities and, if it was possible for them to take steps to resolve the issue, reflect on the impact of their actions. If it is a responsibility, they find the item in the Code that identifies the responsibility and explain what they are required to do. They also submit a half-page reflection on the experience of using the Code and how they might use it in the future.

Graduate Course

The intended audience for this advanced coursework on ethics is students pursuing a graduate degree in early childhood education. The assignment involves students learning to write and analyze an ethical dilemma that they have experienced using the case analysis framework outlined in Chapter 5, pages 57–60.

The amount of time dedicated to this assignment will depend on the structure of the program, the course in which it is taught, and the students' prior knowledge of the NAEYC Code of Ethical Conduct. Developing skill in ethical analysis is demanding, and several class sessions will be needed to introduce the case analysis method, to help the students identify an ethical dilemma, and to work through the process of finding a defensible resolution to that dilemma. This assignment can be used as a Key Assessment to address Standard 6b of NAEYC Standards for Early Childhood Professional Preparation: "Knowing about and upholding ethical standards and other professional guidelines." A rubric evaluating students' success can be found in Chapter 7 on pages 89–90.

Objectives

The objectives for this advanced ethics assignment are for students to

- Demonstrate their ability to identify and clearly describe a real-life ethical dilemma
- Apply the NAEYC Code of Ethical Conduct to the dilemma
- Arrive at a justifiable resolution to the dilemma
- Apply ethical theory to the resolution they propose to the dilemma
- Thoughtfully reflect on the process of using the NAEYC Code to address a real-life ethical dilemma

The assignment

Students begin the assignment by describing an ethical dilemma they have experienced using the process described in Activity 5.7: Writing an Ethical Dilemma (see Chapter 5, page 61). Once they have completed that process successfully, they analyze their dilemma following the process described in Activity 5.6: Analyzing an Ethical Dilemma (see Chapter 5, page 61).

The assignment can be expanded for advanced students by adding these two additional components:

- A short description of how ethical theories (described in Chapter 5 of this book, and in more detail in *Ethics and the Early Childhood Educator*, Chapter 3, pages 31–32) can be used as a lens to reflect on the implications of various resolutions to their dilemma.
- A final reflection that includes
  - » Why they chose the resolution they selected
  - » How the NAEYC Code was, or was not, helpful
  - » The extent to which they needed to use professional judgment in addition to items in the Code to resolve the dilemma
  - » How ethical theory helped them identify the most defensible resolution to this dilemma
  - » What they learned about ethical decision making and using a code of ethics

Sequence of instruction

Described below is a sequence of class sessions that were taught as part of a graduate course on ethics and professionalism. The ethical analysis was the final assignment for the course. The edited version of the case and its analysis were placed in the portfolio that students completed as the culminating assignment in the master's program.

Duration: Five 2½-hour class sessions on ethics were taught as part of the course. Students had had a brief introduction to ethics and morality in a previous course.

Preparation: Prior to the first class session, ask the students to submit descriptions of some ethical issues they have encountered in their workplace. Provide feedback to help them identify situations that do not involve ethics and to help them differentiate ethical responsibilities from ethical dilemmas. Be sure that each student is ready to enter the first class with ideas for several ethical dilemmas that they can analyze.

Outline of the class sessions

Class 1—Introduction

- The same as Part I of the Advanced Practicum assignment above.
- Activity 5.3: Is This an Ethical Responsibility or an Ethical Dilemma? (see Chapter 5, page 56).

Class 2—Selecting an ethical dilemma to analyze

- In small groups, each student shares the possible dilemmas for analysis that she or he has identified prior to the class and receives feedback from the group and you (the instructor) about which might work best for the assignment. (Move from group to group and offer clarification and assistance as needed.)

■ By the end of the class, students should have selected the dilemma they plan to analyze.

■ Homework: Students write a first draft of their dilemma (Activity 5.7 in Chapter 5, page 61).

Class 3—Describing dilemmas clearly

■ Students share and discuss their drafts in small groups and receive feedback from you and group members to aid in writing a final version of their dilemma.

■ Introduce and discuss the case analysis framework found in Chapter 5, pages 57–60.

■ Homework: Students use feedback from the members of their small group and from you to write a clear description of the dilemma they will analyze. They begin work on the analysis of their dilemma by identifying the conflicting responsibilities involved in it and brainstorming some possible resolutions.

Class 4—Analyzing ethical dilemmas

■ Have students work in small groups to analyze their dilemmas. Ask each student to share
   » The stakeholders
   » The early childhood educator's conflicting responsibilities
   » Possible resolutions
   » Ways that ethical finesse might be used to address the dilemma
   » Items of the NAEYC Code that apply to the dilemma
   » The justifiable resolution they have chosen

■ Structure the groups to encourage productive discussion and ask questions that encourage students to think deeply about their dilemma and their proposed resolution (see pages 64–65 in Chapter 5).

■ Homework: Students complete a first draft of their ethical analysis based on the feedback they received from their small group.

Class 5—Wrap-Up

■ Have students share how they applied ethical theory to their proposed resolutions (see pages 16–20 in Chapter 2 and pages 31–32 in *Ethics and the Early Childhood Educator* for short descriptions of ethical theories).

■ In small groups, have students discuss what they have gained by using the Code and the case analysis framework to address a real-life dilemma. If time permits, they can summarize this small group discussion when they report back to the large group.

■ Homework: Students use feedback from their peers and from you to continue to refine their dilemma and its analysis until it is suitable for inclusion in their final portfolio.

Seven

Assessing Learning and Evaluating Teaching Effectiveness

The real measure of your success in teaching about professional ethics is students' increased competence in resolving the real-life dilemmas in the workplace. Although it is difficult, if not impossible, to measure the impact in the work arena, it is possible to assess students' learning and evaluate your teaching efforts.

This final chapter of *Teaching the NAEYC Code of Ethical Conduct: A Resource Guide* focuses on two dimensions of teaching ethics—assessing participants' learning and evaluating the effectiveness of your teaching. Whenever you teach a session on ethics, you will want to determine if the learners gained the awareness, understanding, and skills that you planned for. If you are leading a conference session or one-time workshop, you will use informal approaches to assess participants' learning. In other instances, such as when ethics is a major topic in a college course, or when you are teaching a series of professional development workshops, it is important to determine how well learners mastered the content and skills you have taught. You will also want to evaluate the appropriateness of the content for the learners, and determine the effectiveness of your format, presentation techniques, and activities. Did the participants in your session, class, or workshop think that their time was well spent and that you helped them to think more clearly about the ethical dimensions of their work? Your approach to gathering this information and how you measure success will depend on your particular circumstances. The following suggestions may help you consider how to approach this task.

Assessing Learning

What did you want participants to learn from the conference presentation, professional development or class session, or seminar you devoted to ethics? Effective evaluation begins by revisiting your objectives and thinking about how you will determine if you achieved them.

Was it your intention for conference participants to learn about the NAEYC Code of Ethical Conduct so that they would pursue future opportunities to study and practice its application? Were you aiming to help preservice teachers become sensitive to the unique responsibilities of those who work with young children? Did you want to help the learners realize they will face ethical issues that do not have clear-cut, easily reached resolutions? Were you providing an in-service workshop for a center's staff to provide them a foundation for ongoing professional discussions of the ethical dimensions of their work that they plan to explore together? Or were you focused on helping graduate students become adept at articulating their processes of ethical decision making? The answers to these questions will inform how you will assess the learning that occurred.

Surveying Participants

Even if you have a limited amount of time to lead a conversation about ethics, as in a conference session, you will still want to encourage participants to reflect upon your presentation and identify what they have learned. These are some strategies that could help you evaluate their learning and your effectiveness when presenting at a conference or other short session.

Strategy 1: Debriefing. When you conduct a session, build in some time for a debriefing. Have participants respond to the following kinds of questions either individually or with a partner, and report their responses back to the whole group.

- What is the most important thing you learned in today's session?
- What will you remember from this session?
- What did you learn that you would like to share with your family and friends, coteacher, or director?
- Would you recommend that a colleague or friend attend this session, class, or workshop? Why or why not?
- What is the next step you will take to become ethically competent?

Strategy 2: Open-ended feedback. If you have a little more time, you can conduct an informal written evaluation. Asking participants to complete sentences like those that follow will provide useful insights into what they gained from your session.

- This discussion of professional ethics has made me more aware of

  _____
- I will not forget _____
- The most important thing I learned was _____
- I would like to know more about _____
- I am still confused about _____
- I feel more confident and ethically competent, because now I

  _____

Statements like these can also be built into more formal evaluations, such as course evaluations and final reflection papers.

Strategy 3: Rating scales. Another assessment strategy is to re-create the continuum below on paper (easel paper works well) and hang it on the wall. Participants place their initials on the continuum before the session begins, and again when it is over. This gives trainees an opportunity to reflect on what they have learned and gives you an indication of whether or not you achieved your goals.

An alternative is to provide a similar continuum for each participant. Ask each participant to place her or his initials at the appropriate point on the continuum before the session begins, and again when it is over.

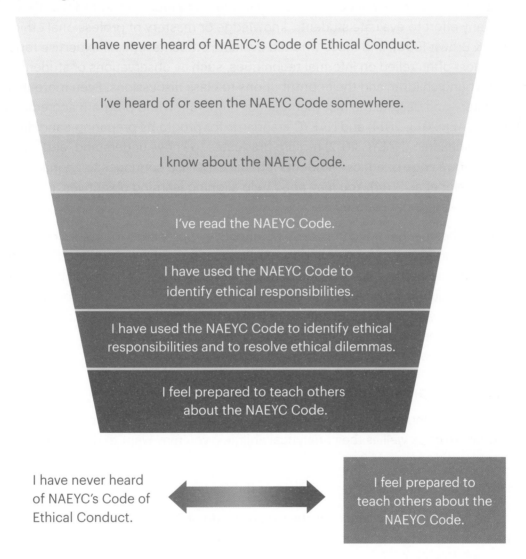

I have never heard of NAEYC's Code of Ethical Conduct.

I've heard of or seen the NAEYC Code somewhere.

I know about the NAEYC Code.

I've read the NAEYC Code.

I have used the NAEYC Code to identify ethical responsibilities.

I have used the NAEYC Code to identify ethical responsibilities and to resolve ethical dilemmas.

I feel prepared to teach others about the NAEYC Code.

I have never heard of NAEYC's Code of Ethical Conduct.

I feel prepared to teach others about the NAEYC Code.

Strategy 4: Reflections. The reflection questions included in this book and in *Ethics and the Early Childhood Educator* are useful resources. As noted in the preceding chapters, you can have students address them as the topic for a journal entry or you can use them as a small group activity. You may add additional questions to highlight particular awareness, information, or skill you want your participants or college students to acquire.

Assessing Ethical Expertise

Informal, ungraded assessment strategies such as open-ended questions that ask for reflections and impressions can give you useful information about learners' attitudes and their level of engagement with ethics, but they do not provide the kind of evidence of learning needed in college and university settings. College teachers have a responsibility to assess students' learning and translate their evaluations into grades.

But measuring students' learning about ethics is neither easy nor precise. Of those teacher educators who responded to a survey in 1995, 14 percent reported that they did not make any effort to evaluate students' knowledge or mastery of professional ethics (Freeman & Brown 1996), and those who did evaluate students' ethical expertise reported that they most often relied on informal techniques, such as observations of students' work with young children and their contributions to class discussions. Even more than 20 years later—and despite the fact that teacher preparation and program accreditation standards (CAEP 2013, 2014) and NAEYC standards for programs preparing candidates to teach young children (NAEYC 2012) require graduates to know, understand, and uphold their profession's code of ethics—students' ethical expertise continues to be inadequately assessed (Keefer et al. 2014). You may need help aligning learning objectives, instructional activities, and assessment strategies.

It is essential that teacher educators develop effective approaches for assessing students' success in learning about and applying the NAEYC Code of Ethical Conduct. Students benefit from assessments that provide accurate information about how well they have mastered the required knowledge and skills, and you benefit from information that can help you make informed adjustments to your instructional strategies (Keefer et al. 2014). Described below are some assessment strategies that may help you gauge how successful you have been in achieving your instructional goals.

An Objective Approach to Assessing Students

If you want to develop an objective approach to evaluating students' knowledge of professional ethics as well as their analytical abilities, you may want to design quizzes or tests to address these goals.

The following are some basic questions about the Code:

- Who is the intended audience for the NAEYC Code of Ethical Conduct? (This can be structured for a short answer or designed as a multiple-choice question.)
- Early childhood educators' responsibilities to what four constituencies are described in the NAEYC Code? (This can be structured for a short answer or designed as a multiple-choice question.)
- The Code's first Principle (P-1.1) "has precedence over all others in this Code." What does it require? Restate the Principle in your own words.

The following are some questions that involve more knowledge and require some application:

- The NAEYC Code does not provide answers to every dilemma an early childhood educator is likely to face. How can it be useful even in situations it does not specifically address?

- The Code has been called "a living document." What does this tell you about the process of its development and revision?

- What are some of the first things you would do when facing a problem that has no right answer? For example, think about the dilemma the teacher faced when a mother asked that her 4-year-old son not nap at school, because when he napped he couldn't fall asleep at a reasonable time at night and had trouble getting up in the morning.

- Present an ethical dilemma (see the "Selected Cases" on pages 143–151 in the Appendix) and a list of four or five of the Code's Principles. Ask students to select the Principle(s) that are relevant to this situation. Have them describe two or three courses of action that could help resolve the dilemma.

- The Code is useful because it identifies ethical responsibilities and guides practitioners' decision making when they face ethical dilemmas. What is the difference between an *ethical responsibility* and an *ethical dilemma*? Give an example of each.

- You frequently overhear a teacher yelling at her class, talking harshly to children, and even threatening them that if they don't "play nicely" she will call their parents and send them home. Do you have an ethical responsibility in this situation? If so, what is your responsibility? Are you faced with an ethical dilemma? If so, what is the dilemma?

Subjective Approaches to Assessing Students

In some instances, you may want to evaluate students' responses to subjective questions that require them to apply their knowledge of professional ethics.

As discussed in Chapter 5, it is worthwhile to have students analyze a workplace problem using the case analysis framework described on pages 57–60. Using a case analysis framework has been shown to "expand candidates' ethical sensitivity toward ill-structured classroom events . . . [and leads them to consider] multiple means of problem solving" (Johnson, Vare, & Evers 2013, 103).

If students are novices, it will be most effective to have them analyze the cases in the Appendix of this book, or those in *Ethics and the Early Childhood Educator* or in other NAEYC publications. When you evaluate students' case analyses, consider how successfully they identified the ethical issues and the stakeholders, and determine if they applied appropriate sections of the Code to find a defensible resolution. You will also need to decide if they appropriately prioritized stakeholders' interests and expressed the choices they made clearly and convincingly. You can use a rubric (see pages 87–88 and

89–90 of this chapter for examples) as a systematic approach for evaluating students' work. Students' work could also be used to document their mastery of several of NAEYC's Standards for Early Childhood Professional Preparation, particularly the following elements of Standard 6: Becoming a Professional.

6b. Knowing about and upholding ethical standards and other professional guidelines

6c. Engaging in continuous, collaborative learning to inform practice

6d. Integrating knowledgeable, reflective, and critical perspectives on early education

More advanced students can describe and analyze an ethical dilemma they have encountered in the course of their work with young children and families. Guidelines for writing a dilemma are found in Activity 5.7 (see Chapter 5, page 61). Students' ability to write a case gives you an indication of their skill differentiating a dilemma from a responsibility, and their ability to appreciate the ethical dimensions embedded in the complex realities faced by early childhood educators. The second part of the assignment for advanced students is to have them analyze the dilemma using the case analysis framework, which can be assessed by the rubric on the pages that follow. It may be best to divide this project into two phases, because even sophisticated students sometimes have difficulty identifying a situation that is a true ethical dilemma. While they might go through the motions of applying the analysis process, doing so if their scenario is not a dilemma can be confusing and nonproductive.

Educators seeking additional information about how to evaluate students' ethical expertise, including their skill of analyzing ethical dilemmas, may find it helpful to refer to the works of Muriel Bebeau (l993), Matthew Keefer and his colleagues (2014), and the book edited by Matthew Sanger and Richard Osguthorpe (2013). Complete citations for these works are included in the References section of this book.

Keefer and his colleagues (2014) also stress the importance of evaluating students' work and providing formative feedback on their efforts to analyze realistic scenarios involving ethical issues. They report that the quality of students' responses improved when the criteria used to evaluate their work were clear and explicit.

Examples of Rubrics Used to Assess Students' Performance

The rubrics that follow are designed to evaluate how well students addressed the objectives identified in the assignments that required them to identify and analyze ethical issues. Those assignments can be used as Key Assessments to address Standard 6b of

NAEYC Standards for Early Childhood Professional Preparation: "Knowing about and upholding ethical standards and other professional guidelines."

■ **Figure 7.1 Rubric for Identifying and Analyzing an Ethical Issue in an Advanced Practicum or Student Teaching Seminar**

(This assignment is on page 76 in Chapter 6 of this book.)

Expert	Proficient	Less proficient than expected
Identifying an ethical issue		
Identified a possible ethical issue, described it effectively to the group, and made substantial contributions to the process of determining if it was an ethical issue.	Made meaningful contributions to the discussion when a possible ethical issue was brought to the group, and contributed to the process of determining if it was an ethical issue.	Was present during the discussion when a possible ethical issue was brought to the group, but participated very little or not at all in the process of determining if it was an ethical issue.
Identifying the stakeholders in an ethical issue		
When discussing an ethical issue, went directly to the section(s) of the Code relevant to identifying its stakeholders.	When discussing an ethical issue, needed help to identify the section(s) of the Code relevant to identifying its stakeholders.	Listened to others identify section(s) of the Code relevant to identifying the stakeholders in the ethical issue being discussed.
Determining if the ethical issue under discussion is a responsibility or a dilemma		
Independently used the Code to determine whether the issue being discussed was an ethical responsibility or an ethical dilemma. Relied on relevant Principles in the Code to justify their perspective.	Could identify, with prompting, the relevant items in the Code that helped determine whether the issue being discussed was an ethical responsibility or an ethical dilemma.	Stated that the issue being discussed was a responsibility or a dilemma without relying on the Code.

Expert	Proficient	Less proficient than expected
Reliance on the Code to resolve a workplace issue		
Relied on specific items in the Code to propose a response to the issue being discussed that was ethically defensible and in the best interests of children and families.	Proposed a response to the issue being discussed that was in the best interests of children and families, but did not rely on the Code to determine its appropriateness.	Proposed a response to the issue being discussed that simply followed the rules. Showed no reliance on the Code.
Deciding on a course of action		
Made substantive contributions to the group's deliberations and participated in reaching an agreement about the most appropriate course of action to address the issue being discussed.	Listened attentively to the group's deliberations, made minor contributions, and agreed with the proposed course of action to address the issue being discussed.	Was not very engaged or not present for these deliberations.
Reflection on the role of the Code of Ethics		
Reflection thoughtfully addressed the contribution the Code made to the resolution of the issue and to the work of early childhood educators.	Reflection mentioned the contribution the Code made to addressing the issue and to the work of early childhood educators.	Reflection did not clearly acknowledge the role of the Code.

◾ Figure 7.2 Rubric for Writing and Analyzing an Ethical Dilemma in a Graduate Course

(This assignment is on page 78 in Chapter 6 of this book.)

Expert	Proficient	Less proficient than expected
Identifies an ethical dilemma, the stakeholders involved, and the early childhood educator's conflicting responsibilities		
Clearly describes an ethical dilemma. Identifies all stakeholders and all of the early childhood educator's conflicting responsibilities.	Clearly describes an ethical dilemma and some ethical issues involved. Identifies most of the stakeholders and/or most of the early childhood educator's conflicting responsibilities.	Does not clearly describe an ethical dilemma. Does not identify most of the stakeholders or identify the early childhood educator's conflicting responsibilities.
Considers alternative courses of action in response to the case		
Recommends a variety of courses of action that balance the early childhood educator's conflicting responsibilities. The suggested resolutions address the concerns of all relevant stakeholders.	Recommends a course of action that addresses more than one conflicting responsibility effectively. The suggested resolution addresses the concerns of more than one stakeholder.	The recommended courses of action do not address one or more of the early childhood educator's responsibilities effectively and/or do not adequately address the concerns of the stakeholders.
Considers ethical finesse		
Demonstrates a clear understanding of ethical finesse and how to apply it thoughtfully to this dilemma.	An understanding of ethical finesse seems clear, but its application to this dilemma is not adequate.	Does not demonstrate an understanding of ethical finesse or apply it to this dilemma.
Looks for guidance in the NAEYC Code		
Identifies many applicable items found in the Code's Core Values, Ideals, and Principles.	Identifies some of the applicable items found in the Code's Core Values, Ideals, and Principles.	Fails to identify the most applicable items found in the Code's Core Values, Ideals, and Principles.

Expert	Proficient	Less proficient than expected
Prioritizes the guidance provided by the Code to decide on a justifiable course of action		
Prioritizes the applicable Core Values, Ideals, and Principles to support a course of action that is clearly justifiable.	Prioritizes the applicable Core Values, Ideals, and Principles to present a course of action that could be justifiable.	Fails to prioritize applicable Core Values, Ideals, and Principles in a way that supports a justifiable course of action.
Personal reflection		
Personal reflection thoughtfully addresses why the identified resolution was justified, the contributions the Code made to the resolution, what was learned about ethical decision making, and the importance of relying on a code of ethics.	Personal reflection touches on why the identified resolution was justified, the contributions of the Code, what was learned about ethical decision making, and the importance of relying on a code of ethics, but lacks specificity.	Personal reflection does not adequately address why the identified resolution was selected, the contribution of the Code, what was learned about ethical decision making, or the importance of relying on a code of ethics.
Clarity of expression and quality of writing		
Descriptions of the dilemma, the analysis, and how ethical theory was applied are thorough and thoughtful. Very well written and organized.	Descriptions of the dilemma, the analysis, and how ethical theory was applied are clear. Well written and organized.	Descriptions of the dilemma, the analysis, and the how ethical theory was applied are incomplete or not clear. Poorly organized, incorrect grammar.

Based on Keefer et al. (2014)

Do Students Take Ethics Into Their Workplace?

Helping students translate theory into practice is the real objective of ethics instruction. But evaluating the success of your efforts is a difficult task. Documenting appropriate uses of the Code in the unpredictable, highly charged, and sensitive circumstances of real-life practice is much more difficult than assessing students' knowledge of the Code in a course or workshop.

One teacher educator responding to the 1995 survey noted, "How much students retain in the field is hard to know" (Freeman & Brown 1996, 10). That response highlights the fact that it is hard to count on seeing evidence of students' ability to apply the Code during visits to their classrooms, or to rely on journal entries or responses on tests to capture the judgment and decision making that occur in real-life situations. These are undoubtedly some of the reasons that so many early childhood teacher educators report that they rely on their observations and instincts rather than on formal assessment tools to evaluate students' ethical expertise. The most effective thing to do is to be alert to opportunities to document any observable evidence that your students are growing into fair, equitable, and ethical professionals, and that they demonstrate the "courage, competence, and confidence to resolve ill-structured, ethical dilemma(s) regardless of distraction or discouragement" (Johnson, Vare, & Evers 2013, 101).

Self-Assessment and Professional Portfolios

For adults who are setting their own learning goals, you can design assessments to help practitioners document and gauge their growing professional competence. Because continued employment, increased compensation, and opportunities for career advancement are often tied to professional development, practitioners may be required to provide proof of their learning to retain a credential or advance in their careers.

How can practitioners assess and document their ethical competence in the workplace? A test, whether addressing basic knowledge or analytical and problem-solving skills, does not reflect the real world. An alternative assessment strategy is for teachers to include in their professional portfolios evidence of how they apply the Code when facing real-life ethical issues.

Practitioners can use the following to verify their ethical knowledge and skill:

- **Document their training.** Offer to provide a single-page description of your ethics workshop, workshop series, or course that can be included in a practitioner's portfolio. Include its title, a summary of its content, and the level of the training (beginner, midlevel, or advanced); the sponsor of the training; the date and duration of the training; and your name, title, and qualifications.
- **Document their learning.** Practitioners can include one of the assessments described in this chapter to provide evidence of their learning about ethics.
- **Document their competence.** Encourage participants to use written self-reflections in the form of journal or diary entries to document the ways they have addressed the ethical responsibilities and dilemmas they encounter in their work. Selected entries (with the names of specific children, families, colleagues, and programs blocked out) can be used as part of a portfolio to demonstrate ethical competence.
- **Document their participation in trainings and application plans.** Provide participants with an easy-to-use format, such as the Training Documentation and Action Plan on the following page, to document the trainings they have attended and their plans for implementing what they have learned.

Training Documentation and Action Plan

Course or workshop title

_____

Date(s), number of sessions, and duration of training(s)

_____

Training sponsor

_____

Presenter's name and qualifications

_____

Level of training: Beginning, intermediate, advanced

_____

Description of the training*

_____

_____

_____

My Action Plan

As a result of what I have learned in this training, I plan to integrate the following action(s) into my practice:

1.

2.

3.

I plan to document my action(s) in the following ways:

1.

2.

3.

*An example of a description of the training: A two-hour workshop designed to acquaint participants with the NAEYC Code of Ethical Conduct. Participants were given an overview of the Code, opportunities to interact with the Code, and practice using the Code to identify ethical responsibilities and to select ethical responses to dilemmas.

Evaluating Teaching

While it is important to use good strategies for assessing what students learned in your ethics training sessions, you should also evaluate the effectiveness of your teaching. This process begins with candid reflection and self-evaluation.

First, think about your preparation. Did you identify your objectives for the presentation, master the content, study your notes, plan effective presentation strategies (including materials for any activities), and preview your delivery before you began? Next, reflect on the learning experiences you provided. How well did you capture the audience's attention? For example, did the personal examples elicit smiles of recognition and nods of agreement? Did your questions launch lively conversations? Did participants actively engage in the activities you had planned, and did they appear to be learning from their participation? Did participants raise insightful questions that showed they understood and were thinking about the information that was presented?

In addition to reflecting on the effectiveness of instruction, you can ask participants for specific feedback about your teaching. Ask them if the activities and discussion questions helped them understand and be prepared to apply the Code to their work with young children. Students could answer these questions in small groups, or you can include them in a written evaluation at the end of your ethics session.

If you carefully consider the responses you receive to the following questions and reflect on your observations about how the training went, you are likely to gain the information you need to help you continually refine your teaching.

- Did the learners indicate they had acquired at least one important concept or fact from the session or class?
- Did the learners indicate they would remember what you consider to be the "big ideas" from the session or class?
- Did the learners actively engage in the games or activities designed to help them learn more about the NAEYC Code and its application?
- Did the learners indicate they would recommend that a colleague or friend should attend this session/class or workshop and why they thought so?
- Did the learners indicate that parts of the session should be changed or eliminated in the future?
- Did the learners indicate they were ready to take an appropriate next step to become ethically competent?

Final Thoughts

Learning about ethics is never finished, because ethical deliberation is a one-on-one, case-by-case process. Developing and refining the skills involved in moral reasoning are ongoing endeavors. Ethical behavior requires careful thought and reflection, pride and humility, a willingness to change, and the courage to remain steadfast. Karl D. Hostetler (1997) observed that "Ethics need not, and probably should not, always be at the forefront of teachers' minds. But it persists as a background project, as teachers are continually searching for . . . what is ethically right and good" (195–196).

We hope you find the resources in this book helpful in preparing early childhood educators with the knowledge, skills, and dispositions they need to apply the NAEYC Code in their work with young children and families. Until we develop ways to assess teachers' classroom behaviors, we will need to rely on observations to know what effect our teaching has had. It is our fervent hope, however, that based on your teaching, ethical practice will increasingly be woven into the everyday fabric of all classrooms serving young children.

Appendix

This Appendix contains reproducible items that accompany the activities described in Chapters 1, 3, 4, and 5. It also contains a collection of cases.

Chapter 1 Teaching Resources

Activity 1.1: Match-Ups

When you were a child	Your answer	Someone whose answer matches
How old were you when you first went to school?		
How many sisters did you have?		
What did you want to be when you grew up?		
What was your least favorite vegetable?		
How many brothers did you have?		
What was your favorite place to play?		
What were you afraid of?		
What was your favorite toy?		
What embarrassed you the most?		
What was your favorite film or TV show?		
What did you think was the worst thing you could do?		

Teaching the NAEYC Code of Ethical Conduct: A Resource Guide. Copyright © 2016 by NAEYC.

Activity 1.2: Scavenger Hunt

Find someone who . . .	Initials	Interesting/Unexpected related fact
loves cats		
loves dogs		
grows vegetables		
teaches 3-year-olds		
went to high school in the '80s		
went to high school in the '00s		
performed in a musical		
likes to sail		
has served on a jury		
is the parent of a young child		
has lived in another country		
speaks a language other than English		
has read all the Narnia or Harry Potter books, or all the books in the *A Series of Unfortunate Events*		
has been president (of anything)		
loves to cook		

Activity 1.3: BINGO

B	I	N	G	O
is a cat owner	is a dog owner	has a vegetable garden	teaches 3-year-olds	teaches 4-year-olds
taught infants or toddlers	taught kindergarten	went to high school in the last century	went to high school in this century	is the parent of a young child
performed in a musical	owns an iPad	served on a jury	lived in another country	speaks a language other than English
read all the Harry Potter books	has been president (of anything)	made jam	traveled to another continent	made pasta from scratch
traveled somewhere by train	sews, knits, or crochets	surfs or skis	rides a bike to work	doesn't drive

Chapter 3 Teaching Resources

Activity 3.5: My Gift to Children

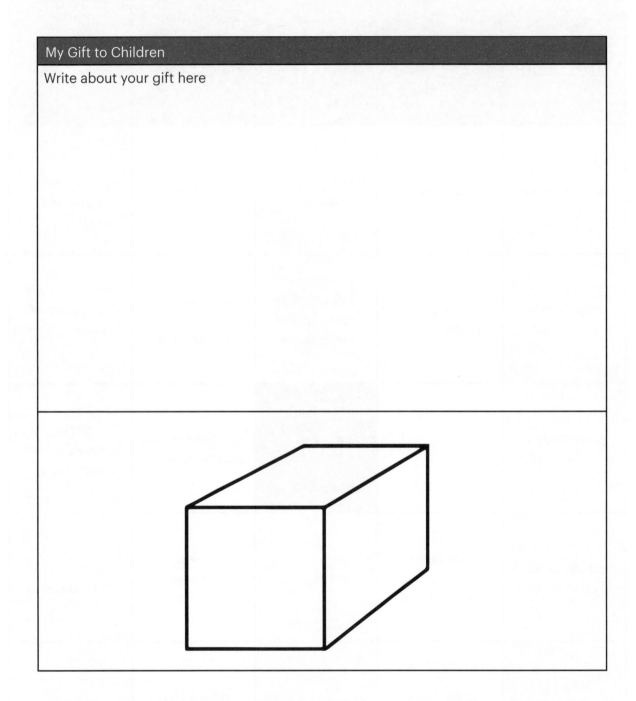

Adapted by permission, from S. Nolte, *PACE (Professional and Career Education for Early Childhood) Training Manual for ED 140,* revised edition (Honolulu, HI: Honolulu Community College, 1998).

Teaching the NAEYC Code of Ethical Conduct: A Resource Guide. Copyright © 2016 by NAEYC.

Activity 3.6: Variation 1 on The Wall of Personal Values: Personal Values Continua

Personal Values Continua
Mark where your beliefs fall along each continuum

| Strongly Agree | | | Strongly Disagree |

It is better to do good than to be wealthy.

| Strongly Agree | | | Strongly Disagree |

It is more important to be smart
than to be good or moral.

| Strongly Agree | | | Strongly Disagree |

It is okay to lie under certain circumstances.

| Strongly Agree | | | Strongly Disagree |

Following your own conscience is more important
than doing what others want you to do.

| Strongly Agree | | | Strongly Disagree |

It is important to follow the law
even if you disagree with it.

| Strongly Agree | | | Strongly Disagree |

It is okay to steal if your family
really needs something.

| Strongly Agree | | | Strongly Disagree |

Family responsibilities are more important than
responsibilities to yourself or your employer.

| Strongly Agree | | | Strongly Disagree |

People need formal religious institutions to help
them determine what is right and wrong.

| Strongly Agree | | | Strongly Disagree |

Society does not have the right to dictate how people
will raise, care for, or educate their children.

| Strongly Agree | | | Strongly Disagree |

As a society, we have the right and responsibility
to ban harmful substances and devices.

| Strongly Agree | | | Strongly Disagree |

As a society, we have the responsibility to make
sure that all peoples' basic needs are met.

| Strongly Agree | | | Strongly Disagree |

No price is too great to preserve our environment.

| Strongly Agree | | | Strongly Disagree |

It is never okay to take a life.

Teaching the NAEYC Code of Ethical Conduct: A Resource Guide. Copyright © 2016 by NAEYC.

Activity 3.7: Sources of Values

What I value	Source of the value
☐ Education	
☐ Beauty	
☐ Religion	
☐ Competence	
☐ Creativity	
☐ Doing good	
☐ Excitement and stimulation	
☐ Family	
☐ Financial well-being	
☐ Friendship	
☐ Happiness	
☐ Honesty	
☐ Health	
☐ Intellectual curiosity	
☐ Meaningful work	
☐ The natural environment	
☐ Order	
☐ Peace	

Activity 3.8 and Activity 3.9: Values Cards

The choices we make about what we value are personal. The 35 reproducible signs that follow are one collection of values. You can expand this collection to reflect even greater cultural, geographical, and experiential diversity or to include ideas from a list that students brainstorm.

These signs are designed to be used for Activity 3.8: Values Auction and Activity 3.9: Values Sort on page 30 in Chapter 3.

If you will be using them for the Values Auction, it will be helpful to make duplicates and triplicates to ensure active and comparative bidding during the activity.

beauty	the arts	adventure
comfort	children	charity
creativity	competence	community

fairness	freedom	health
education	family	happiness
diversity	faith	friendship

honesty & integrity	individuality	knowledge
heritage & culture	independence	kindness & compassion
helping others	humor	intellect

meaningful work	loyalty	life
respect for others	order	natural environment
	success	spirituality

Activity 3.14: The Wall of Professional Values

Professional Values Continua
Mark where your beliefs fall along each continuum

Strongly Agree			Strongly Disagree

A teacher's most important task is to help children feel good about themselves.

Strongly Agree			Strongly Disagree

Children who attend preschool and kindergarten should learn the discipline that they will need later in school.

Strongly Agree			Strongly Disagree

Children won't learn unless the teacher tells them what to do.

Strongly Agree			Strongly Disagree

Development of intellectual skills is the most important task of an early childhood program.

Strongly Agree			Strongly Disagree

Given enough time and equipment, children will learn all they need without traditional, intentional teaching.

Strongly Agree			Strongly Disagree

Children should be allowed to play in school.

Strongly Agree			Strongly Disagree

Families should not be allowed to interfere in their child's learning at school.

Strongly Agree			Strongly Disagree

To be fair, all children should be treated the same way in school.

Strongly Agree			Strongly Disagree

It is important for teachers to be responsive to the individual needs and interests of all children.

Strongly Agree			Strongly Disagree

It is appropriate for educators to use rewards to help change children's behaviors.

Strongly Agree			Strongly Disagree

Early childhood curriculum should be based on what children will need to know later in school.

Strongly Agree			Strongly Disagree

Children who misbehave should not be allowed special privileges.

Strongly Agree			Strongly Disagree

It is important for children [choose an age group] to learn to color within and cut on the lines, write neatly, stand in line, and use proper punctuation.

Teaching the NAEYC Code of Ethical Conduct: A Resource Guide. Copyright © 2016 by NAEYC.

Activity 3.16: Is It a Profession?

Criteria for Professional Status

1. A profession has a *specialized body of knowledge and expertise* that is based on theory and is applied according to the particular needs of each case.

2. A profession requires practitioners to participate in *prolonged training* based on principles that involve judgment for their application (not a precise set of behaviors that apply in all cases).

3. A profession has rigorous *requirements for entry* into training that are controlled by members of the profession. Training is delivered in accredited institutions. Graduation from an accredited program is necessary, but professionals may also need to take an examination in order to receive a license to practice.

4. Members of the profession have agreed on *standards of practice*—recommended procedures for dealing with situations that are regularly encountered in the workplace. A professional must be aware of and be guided by the standards of practice, but the decision about how to act needs to be responsive to the specifics of a situation.

5. A profession has a *commitment to serving a significant social value*. It provides a service that is essential to society and has as its primary goal, meeting the needs of others. Professions are dedicated to the public interest, altruistic, and service oriented rather than profit oriented.

6. Based on its important function and the specialized knowledge and skill of its practitioners, a profession is recognized as *the only group in the society that can perform its specialized functions*.

7. Because others in the society do not have the technical knowledge required to oversee their work, professions are characterized by *autonomy*—self-governance that results in internal control over the quality of the services provided.

8. A profession has a *code of ethics* that assures members of the society that it will serve the public good. A code is a document that spells out the profession's moral obligations to society and its guidelines for moral behavior.

From S. Feeney , N.K. Freeman, & P. J. Pizzolongo, *Ethics and the Early Childhood Educator: Using the NAEYC Code,* 2nd ed. (Washington, DC: NAEYC, 2012), 7.

Activity 3.17: Assessing Our Professionalism Scoring Sheet

Assessing Our Professionalism

Criterion	How we measure up
Specialized knowledge and expertise	
Prolonged training	
Rigorous requirements for entry into training	
Standards of practice	
Commitment to serving a significant social value	
The only group that can perform its specialized function	
Autonomy, self-governance	
Code of ethics	

Teaching the NAEYC Code of Ethical Conduct: A Resource Guide. Copyright © 2016 by NAEYC.

Chapter 4 Teaching Resources

Activity 4.5: Is it Ethical? Game

Is It Ethical?

Directions: Each player needs a piece of paper to tally answers and a copy of the NAEYC Code. If you are playing Set B for Program Administrators, you need both the NAEYC Code and the Supplement for Program Administrators.

1. Form small groups of 4–6.

2. Designate a dealer to read the instructions aloud and to shuffle and deal the Situation Cards.

3. The player to the dealer's right reads one of the Situation Cards (including *the issue* and *the response)* aloud to the group.

4. Each player should decide whether the response described on the card is Ethical or Not Ethical, and then record the number of the situation (found on the Situation Card) and "**E**" or "**NE**" without consulting either the Code or others in their group.

5. Players then tell their small group what they decided and why.

6. All players then search the Code for the ethical Principle(s) and/or Ideal(s) that support their decision. They record the number(s) of the supporting item(s) in the Code on their tally sheets.

7. Players then discuss what they have found and attempt to reach an agreement on the Principle(s) and Ideal(s) involved. It is okay for players to change their minds during this discussion. If players cannot agree, the dealer should note this on his or her tally sheet and move on.

8. The next player reads the next situation and play continues in this manner.

9. Play continues until time is called.

When time is called, you will have an opportunity to review the situations your group discussed and find out if you were "right." Sometimes players decide to keep score. Your leader will tell you how to score your answers if you are going to keep score.

1A • The Broken Marriage

You are a family child care provider. A parent of a child in your care confides in you and tells you that she is having marital difficulties. Your best friend, another parent, suspects that this family is having problems. She pumps you for information.

The issue: Do you reveal anything? Do you risk your friendship by refusing OR share the information and swear your friend to secrecy?

Response: You share a little bit! In this community you know that word is going to get around sooner or later; it isn't worth jeopardizing your friendship.

Is It Ethical? • 1A

2A • The Great Assistant

You are a preschool teacher. Finally, after two frustrating years of not having a good assistant teacher, you have a great one. She's reliable, has training, is smart, and is great with kids. Your director comes to you and explains that she has an opening in another class. She asks if you think your assistant might be a good person for the job.

The issue: Do you tell her yes and go back to having lousy help OR say no and know the children's education will be jeopardized? (You know she would do a great job.)

Response: You say, "No, I don't really think she's ready," hoping that the director will find someone else.

Is It Ethical? • 2A

3A • The Aggressive Child

You are a preschool teacher. A large and extremely aggressive 4-year-old boy in your class is frightening and hurting other children. Your director and a mental health specialist have been unable to help. His parents feel that his behavior is typical for boys his age; they won't get counseling. You and your coteacher are becoming stressed and tired, and you are worried that the other children are not getting the attention they need.

The issue: Do you ask the director to expel the child from the center OR do you decide to keep on trying, even though other children are suffering from lack of attention?

Response: You tell the director you cannot keep on working with this child and that you will leave if the child is not removed.

Is It Ethical? • 3A

4A • The Incompetent Teacher

You are a preschool teacher. The teacher in the class next door is not doing a great job. She often comes in without any plans made and borrows activities from you. Her classroom is chaotic, and you have seen children doing things you think are inappropriate, even dangerous.

The issue: Do you confront her even though she might get mad at you and your working environment will be unpleasant OR do you keep on being exploited and knowing kids will suffer?

Response: You let it go; the director is sure to notice sooner or later.

Is It Ethical? • 4A

Teaching the NAEYC Code of Ethical Conduct: A Resource Guide. Copyright © 2016 by NAEYC.

5A • The High-Paying Job

You have just graduated from an early childhood education program. You understand developmentally appropriate practice and the value of play. You take a job working in a child care center near your home and are delighted that it pays well. You are surprised to find that you are expected to have the 3- and 4-year-old children sit for long hours each day and do worksheets. When you question this approach, you are told, "This is how we have always taught, and the teachers and families are very happy with it."

The issue: Do you keep working at a good paying job with a program that isn't good for children OR quit and take a less well-paid job?

Response: You keep the job. Maybe you can change things.

Is It Ethical? • 5A

6A • The Volunteer

A boy in your group of 4-year-olds who is usually cooperative has been irritable. He seldom smiles and frequently quarrels with other children. You mention this to his mother. She tells you she and her husband have been arguing and have decided to divorce. A few days later when you are working with a volunteer, the child spills paint. The volunteer asks the child to help clean it up, but he refuses. She asks him a second time, and he shouts that he will not. He starts screaming and knocks over more paint. During naptime, you and the volunteer sit down for coffee. She is still upset.

The issue: Do you help the volunteer understand the child and breach confidentiality OR keep quiet and risk her misunderstanding?

Response: You tell. It will help her to work with the child.

Is It Ethical? • 6A

7A • The Nap

The mother of a 4-year-old in your class has asked that he not nap at school, because when he naps he stays up too late at night, making it difficult for her to get him up at 5 a.m. so she can get to work. You have observed that he really needs a nap to be able to function in the afternoon.

The issue: Do you respect the mother's wishes and wake him up OR do you tell her no because he needs the nap?

Response: You wake him up. The mother knows what her family needs, and you want to support her.

Is It Ethical? • 7A

8A • Cooking With Children

You are a preschool teacher and have just moved to another state and taken a job. You have always included lots of cooking in your curriculum and believe that it is a great way to motivate children and integrate learning. After your first cooking project in your new job, the director takes you aside and tells you that cooking is against licensing rules in this state because of potential health and safety risks to children.

The issue: Do you follow this regulation even though you believe it's stupid and wrong OR do you do what you believe is best practice?

Response: You stop cooking but express your concern about the policy to your director and ask her to communicate this concern to the licensing authority.

Is It Ethical? • 8A

Teaching the NAEYC Code of Ethical Conduct: A Resource Guide. Copyright © 2016 by NAEYC.

9A • The Divorce

You are the teacher of a 7-year-old whose parents are going through a very contentious divorce. The mother has been a model parent and always helps out in your class. She seems very loving and concerned. The father often comes into school raging and complaining. He is harsh with his child. You have been asked by the child's mother to testify on her behalf in a child custody hearing.

The issue: Do you agree to testify? Do you take the side of one parent over another in a conflict OR do you remain neutral?

Response: You agree to testify. It's obvious that the mother will be a better parent.

Is It Ethical? • 9A

10A • Cultural Differences

You teach in a school that has a population from a culture in which physical punishment is common. This morning a boy from this cultural group strikes another child. A new aide who shares the child's culture grabs him and twists his ear. The child is momentarily stunned but soon is fine and seems calm the rest of the day. Apart from some redness, there are no other effects. When you speak with the aide, she tells you children in her community are used to this discipline. She says, "It calmed him down, didn't it?"

The issue: Do you tell the aide that physical punishment is not acceptable in your class OR do you let it go?

Response: You let it go, because she knows the culture better than you do.

Is It Ethical? • 10A

11A • Contagious Diarrhea

You have been informed that a 2-year old in the next classroom has been diagnosed as having contagious diarrhea. You expect families will be alerted to the illness through a posted notice, but the director of your center has dismissed the problem, only telling teachers to be sure to wear gloves and wash their hands well after changing the child. You go to the director and express your concern. She says she doesn't want to upset the parents and that good hygiene should take care of the problem.

The issue: Do you tell parents or the board of directors of the situation and your concern OR do you assume the director knows what she's doing?

Response: You don't tell; you're afraid that she'll get angry and this will make your work situation unpleasant.

Is It Ethical? • 11A

12A • Going Home

You are a kindergarten teacher. A student's mother comes to pick up her child and drive him home. From her slurred speech and clumsy movements, you suspect that she has been drinking heavily.

The issue: Do you refuse to let the parent take the child and ask her to call someone else to drive OR do you let her drive the child home?

Response: You decide to ignore it this time, because you're not sure that she's really drunk.

Is It Ethical? • 12A

13A • The Harsh Teacher

The teacher in the next room has always been harsh with the children. Lately, however, you are becoming increasingly concerned about her open hostility and how angry she gets with the children. You have often heard her belittle the children.

The issue: Do you confront the teacher about her harsh behavior OR do you ignore it?

Response: You ask to meet with her one day after school and tell her about your concerns.

Is It Ethical? • 13A

14A • The Ethnic Joke

You teach in a preschool. One afternoon in the lounge, you hear a coworker make an insulting joke about children and families of a particular ethnic group. It makes you feel uncomfortable, and you think her comments show an unhealthy prejudice. But everyone else laughs.

The issue: Do you risk losing your good relationship with your colleague by saying something OR do you try to ignore it?

Response: You are silent. It would be too embarrassing to confront her.

Is It Ethical? • 14A

15A • The Test

The program where you teach is under pressure to use a new test for monitoring children's progress, and you will receive training on how to administer it. Your director has told you not to bother to collect detailed observations any longer because she does not plan to use them as the primary way to assess children's progress. You have been working with your coteachers to observe and record children's behavior for years, and you're happy with the way your assessment system works to help you plan for each child and the group.

The issue: Do you use the new test in the way that you've been told to OR do you continue to assess children with your current system?

Response: You administer the new test but continue to observe and record children's behavior; you do not tell your director that you are doing so.

Is It Ethical? • 15A

16A • Speaking English

You've been teaching in a multilingual program for many years. You speak English and Spanish, and you use both languages in your classroom. You also have in your group several children who are Chinese and who do not speak English. You've asked their parents to teach you some words in Chinese so that you can help children with routines and in their play—words such as "bathroom" and "lunch." Several parents are concerned that their children will not learn English if you keep speaking other languages the classroom.

The Issue: Do you follow the families' wishes and speak no Chinese in your classroom OR do you integrate Chinese into your classroom to meet the needs of your diverse population?

Response: You include some Chinese words into your classroom and share information with the families about the importance of supporting children's use of their home language as they learn English.

Is It Ethical? • 16A

1B • The Former Colleague

You are the director of a children's center where there is a teacher's job open. A former colleague from another program has applied for the position. She is the most qualified candidate and a great teacher, but you never liked her personally.

The issue: Do you hire someone who is right for the job but not a person you like OR do you choose someone easier to work with?

Response: You hire someone else. It just wouldn't work out.

Is It Ethical? • 1B

2B • The Wealthy Benefactor

You are a preschool director of a prestigious school with a long waiting list. You are fortunate because a wealthy benefactor donates a lot of money to your school each year. The chairman of the board of your program comes to you and explains that the wealthy benefactor's daughter is moving back home with her 2-year-old son. The chairman asks you to immediately enroll the benefactor's grandson.

The issue: Do you do as you are asked and displace a family that has been on the waiting list for a long time OR do you say no and risk the school's funding by offending the benefactor?

Response: You enroll the child as an "overload" in the 2-year-olds class.

Is It Ethical? • 2B

3B • Grandma

You are the director of a child care center. The church in which your program is housed has decided to sponsor adult day care for the elderly. To make room, you will have to close a classroom, reduce enrollment, and lay off staff. You have two choices. You can lay off "Grandma," who is loved by parents and has been with the center for many years. Grandma is only minimally competent by today's standards and does not have training or credentials. Your other choice is to lay off the teacher hired most recently. She is young, well trained, and does a good job in the classroom.

The issue: Do you lay off a more competent and qualified teacher OR the one who is only marginally competent?

Response: You keep Grandma on. The younger teacher will find another job.

Is It Ethical? • 3B

4B • The Broken Building

You are the director of a preschool that serves a community in which many families have low incomes. Your rent is very low, which allows you to charge a very low tuition. Your landlord has let the building fall into dangerous disrepair. There are no other low-rent facilities in the community.

The issue: Do you move to a safer, more expensive facility and raise tuition, which will force some families out, OR do you make the best of it and keep tuition low?

Response: You stay! Families desperately need your program. You and the staff watch the children carefully to make sure that no one gets hurt.

Is It Ethical? • 4B

Teaching the NAEYC Code of Ethical Conduct: A Resource Guide. Copyright © 2016 by NAEYC.

5B • Gossip

You are a preschool director. One day you go to a classroom to give a teacher a message. It's naptime, and you observe two teachers discussing the home life of a child whose father has been arrested for drunk driving.

The issue: Do you tell the teachers that this is not acceptable behavior OR do you let it go and maintain your relationship with the teachers?

Response: You tell them to stop. You can't let gossip flourish in your school.

Is It Ethical? • 5B

6B • The Former Employee

You are a preschool director who hears through the grapevine that a former employee was charged with abusing her own child but was acquitted. You receive a call from another director who says that she is considering hiring the former employee, who has given your name as a reference.

The issue: Do you only share information about her work with you OR do you mention the child abuse charge even though she was acquitted?

Response: You share only what you know through direct experience.

Is It Ethical? • 6B

7B • The Inaccurate Advertisement

You are the director of a child care center. Last year you had a graphic design firm create new brochures, redesign your webpage, and create other promotional materials for your center. They state that your program has earned the highest rating on your state's QRIS. Unfortunately, your program's rating was downgraded because not all of your current teachers have the required training. You think the new brochures and other materials are very effective, and your enrollment has increased since you've been using them.

The issue: Do you stop using the brochures and other materials with incorrect information OR do you continue to use them because they are attractive and were expensive.

Response: You continue to use them. No one has complained about the inaccuracy.

Is It Ethical? • 7B

8B • The Academic Curriculum

You are a center director and have been approached by the corporation that runs your program and asked to use a scripted academic curriculum that takes up most of each morning. This makes you very uncomfortable. Your continued good relationship with your employer and possibly your job are dependent on your agreeing to this request.

The issue: Do you agree, even though you do not believe that this is in the best interests of children OR do you refuse and risk your job?

Response: You agree; you can't afford to lose your job right now.

Is It Ethical? • 8B

Teaching the NAEYC Code of Ethical Conduct: A Resource Guide. Copyright © 2016 by NAEYC.

The Answer Sheet responses are based on the NAEYC Code of Ethical Conduct, revised 2005, reaffirmed and updated 2011. All references (P-2.13, P-3A.3, etc., and the text that follows) are from the Code. The answers for each situation are **E** = Ethical or **NE** = Not Ethical.

Situation 1A—The Broken Marriage. NE. P-2.13—We shall maintain confidentiality and shall respect the family's right to privacy.

Situation 2A—The Great Assistant. NE. P-3A.3—We shall exercise care in expressing views regarding the personal attributes or professional conduct of coworkers. Statements should be based on firsthand knowledge, not hearsay, and relevant to the interests of children and programs. (Participants might also mention I-3A.3—To support coworkers in meeting their professional needs and in their professional development; and I-3A.4—To accord coworkers due recognition of professional achievement.)

Situation 3A—The Aggressive Child. NE. P-1.7—We shall strive to build individual relationships with each child; make individualized adaptations in teaching strategies, learning environments, and curricula; and consult with the family so that each child benefits from the program. If, after such efforts have been exhausted, the current placement does not meet a child's needs, or the child is seriously jeopardizing the ability of other children to benefit from the program, we shall collaborate with the child's family and appropriate specialists to determine the additional services needed and/or the placement option(s) most likely to ensure the child's success.

Situation 4A—The Incompetent Teacher. NE. P-3A.2—When we have a concern about the professional behavior of a coworker, we shall first let that person know of our concern. P-3B.4—If we have concerns about a colleague's behavior, and children's well-being is not at risk, we may address the concern with that individual. If . . . the situation does not improve after it has been brought to the colleague's attention, we shall report the colleague's unethical or incompetent behavior to an appropriate authority.

Situation 5A—The High-Paying Job. E. P-3B.1—When we do not agree with program policies, we shall attempt to effect change through constructive action within the organization.

Situation 6A—The Volunteer. NE. P-2.13—We shall maintain confidentiality and shall respect the family's right to privacy. . . .

Situation 7A—The Nap. *It depends:* **E,** if we determine that it is not harmful to the child. I-2.6—To acknowledge families' childrearing values and their right to make decisions for their children. **NE,** if we determine that it is harmful to the child to be deprived of a nap. P.1.1—Above all, we shall not harm children. We shall not participate in practices that are . . . harmful . . . to children. . . . This principle has precedence over all others in this Code.

Situation 8A—Cooking With Children. E. P-4.8—We shall not participate in practices that are in violation of laws and regulations that protect children in our programs. This teacher might also consider I-4.7: To support policies and laws that promote the well-being of children and families, and to work to change those that impair their well-being. To participate in developing policies and laws that are needed. Also, P-3B.1— We shall follow all program policies. When we do not agree with program policies, we shall attempt to effect change through constructive action within the organization.

Situation 9A—The Divorce. NE. P-2.14—In cases where family members are in conflict, we shall work openly, sharing our observations of the child, to help all parties. . . . We shall refrain from becoming an advocate for one party.

Situation 10A—Cultural Differences. NE. P-1.1—Above all, we shall not harm children. We shall not participate in practices that are . . . physically harmful, disrespectful . . . or intimidating to children. This principle has precedence over all others in this Code. P-1.11—When we become aware of a practice or situation that endangers the health, safety, or well-being of children, we have an ethical responsibility to protect children. P-3A.2—When we have concerns about the professional behavior of a coworker, we shall first let that person know of our concern. P-3B.4—If we have concerns about a colleague's behavior . . . we may address the concern with that individual. If . . . the situation does not improve after it has been brought to the colleague's attention, we shall report the colleague's unethical or incompetent behavior to an appropriate authority.

Situation 11A—Contagious Diarrhea. NE. P-2.9—We shall inform the family of . . . risks such as exposures to contagious disease that may result in infection. P-3B.1—When we do not agree with program policies, we shall attempt to effect change through constructive action within the organization. P-4.9—When we have evidence that an early childhood program is violating laws or regulations protecting children, we shall report the violation to appropriate authorities who can be expected to remedy the situation.

Situation 12A—Going Home. NE. P-1.1—Above all, we shall not harm children. We shall not participate in practices that are . . . physically harmful . . . to children. This principle has precedence over all others in this Code. P-1.11—When we become aware of a . . . situation that endangers the health, safety, or well-being of children, we have an ethical responsibility to protect children.

Situation 13A—The Harsh Teacher. E. P-3A.2—When we have concerns about the professional behavior of a coworker, we shall first let that person know of our concern in a way that shows respect . . . and then attempt to resolve the matter collegially and in a confidential manner. P-3B.4—If we have concerns about a colleague's behavior . . . we may address the concern with that individual. If . . . the situation does not improve after it has been brought to the colleague's attention, we shall report the colleague's unethical or incompetent behavior to an appropriate authority. The overriding issue is P-1.1—Above all, we shall not harm children.

Situation 14A—The Ethnic Joke. NE. P-3A.2—When we have concerns about the professional behavior of a coworker, we shall first let that person know of our concern. Participants might also mention I-2.5—To respect the dignity and preferences of each family . . . its . . . culture, language, customs, and beliefs.

Situation 15A—The Test. NE. P-1.5—We shall use appropriate assessment systems, which include multiple sources of information. P-3B.1—We shall follow all program policies. When we do not agree with program policies, we shall attempt to effect change through constructive action within the organization.

Situation 16A—Speaking English. E. P-1.2—We shall care for and educate children in . . . environments that . . . support each child's culture, language, ethnicity. P-2.2—We shall inform families of program philosophy . . . and explain why we teach as we do. P-4.4— We shall be objective and accurate in reporting the knowledge upon which we base our program practices.

Answer Sheets—Set B
Administrator Focus

The Answer Sheet responses are based on the NAEYC Code of Ethical Conduct: Supplement for Program Administrators (NAEYC 2006). All references (P-2.13, P-3A.3, etc., and the text that follows) are from the Supplement. The answers for each situation are **E** = Ethical or **NE** = Not Ethical.

Situation 1B—The Former Colleague. NE. P-3.13—We shall make hiring, retention, termination, and promotion decisions based solely on a person's competence, record of accomplishment, ability to carry out the responsibilities of the position. . . .

Situation 2B—The Wealthy Benefactor. NE. P-1.3—We shall have clearly stated policies for the respectful treatment of children and adults. P-2.5—We shall develop enrollment policies that clearly describe admission policies and priorities.

Situation 3B—Grandma. NE. P-3.13—We shall make hiring, retention, termination, and promotion decisions based solely on a person's competence, record of accomplishment, ability to carry out the responsibilities of the position, and professional preparation specific to the developmental levels of children in his/her care.

Situation 4B—The Broken Building. *It depends:* **NE,** if you feel that the condition of the building endangers children engaged in typical play. P-1.1—We shall place the welfare and safety of children above other obligations. **E,** if you do not think the condition of the building endangers children. (Note: There are a number of ways to finesse this problem on behalf of children and families, such as fundraising, grant writing, workdays, and negotiation with the landlord.)

Situation 5B—Gossip. E. P-3.9—We shall inform staff whose performance does not meet program expectations of areas of concern.

Situation 6B—The Former Employee. E. P-3.12—In making personnel evaluations and recommendations, we shall make judgments based on fact and relevant to the interests of children and programs. (You state that your comments only give information that is relevant to the position and based on your firsthand observations of the person's work.)

Situation 7B— The Inaccurate Advertisement. NE, P-2.2—We shall provide families with complete and honest information concerning . . . the services provided. P-5.1—We shall communicate openly and truthfully about the nature . . . of services that we provide.

Situation 8B—The Academic Curriculum. *It depends:* **E,** if you do not believe that the new program is harmful to children. **NE,** if you believe that the program will be harmful to children. P-1.1: We shall place the welfare and safety of children above other obligations. (Participants may mention I-1.2—To provide a high-quality program based on current knowledge of child development. . . .)

Chapter 5 Teaching Resources

Activity 5.2: What Kind of Issue Is It?

What Kind of Issue Is It?

Ethical Issues

Situations that involve determining what is right and wrong, rights and responsibilities, and human welfare. They include responsibilities and dilemmas.

Ethical Responsibilities	**Ethical Dilemmas**
Mandates describing what early childhood educators **must** or **must not** do. They describe how early childhood educators are required to act and are clearly spelled out in the Code.	Situations that present conflicting obligations and have more than one possible resolution, each of which can be justified as being an ethical choice.

1. This is an activity for 2–5 participants.

2. Place the three sorting sheets ("This Teacher Is NOT Facing an Ethical Issue." "This Teacher Is Facing an Ethical Responsibility." "This Teacher Is Facing an Ethical Dilemma.") where all can see them.

3. Shuffle the cards and place them in a stack facedown in front of all participants.

4. The first participant picks a card, reads it out loud, and works with the others in the group to decide if it is an ethical issue. If it is not an ethical issue, the participant places it on the "This Teacher Is NOT Facing an Ethical Issue" sorting sheet.

5. If it is an ethical issue, your group needs to answer the question, "Is this an ethical responsibility or is this an ethical dilemma?" Refer to the NAEYC Code and decide with your group. When your group has reached consensus on an answer to that question, place the card on either the "This Teacher Is Facing an Ethical Responsibility" or the "This Teacher Is Facing an Ethical Dilemma" sorting sheet. Continue until all cards have been sorted.

Now Determine If You Have Sorted the Cards Correctly

(Your instructor may lead this part of the activity.)

1. Notice that each card is numbered. These numbers correspond with the number of the case on the What Kind of Issue Is it? Answer Sheet. The Answer Sheet restates each issue, identifies those that are not ethical issues, and notes whether the ethical issues are responsibilities or dilemmas. Use it to see if you sorted the card correctly.

2. If you sorted the card correctly, leave it faceup on its sorting sheet.

3. If you made a mistake, turn the card over.

4. Count how many cards your team sorted correctly. This tells you how well you can differentiate ethical issues from other issues, and how well you understand the difference between an ethical responsibility and an ethical dilemma.

Ethical Issues

Situations that involve determining what is right and wrong, rights and responsibilities, and human welfare. They include responsibilities and dilemmas.

This Teacher is NOT Facing an Ethical Issue

Ethical Responsibilities

Mandates describing what early childhood educators **must** or **must not** do. They describe how early childhood educators are required to act and are clearly spelled out in the Code.

This Teacher is Facing an Ethical Responsibility

Ethical Dilemmas

Situations that present conflicting obligations and have more than one possible resolution, each of which can be justified as being an ethical choice.

This Teacher is Facing an Ethical Dilemma

Teaching the NAEYC Code of Ethical Conduct: A Resource Guide. Copyright © 2016 by NAEYC.

1	2
A child comes in with a hand-shaped bruise on his face.	A teacher discovers a fruiting hot chili pepper growing in the play yard.
3	**4**
A teacher is required to administer a paper-and-pencil test to all the 4-year-olds in his class at the same time. Results will be used to place children in kindergarten.	A regular volunteer saw a 4-year-old having a difficult day. He was very aggressive and cried often. She asked the teacher what was going on. The teacher knows his parents are in the middle of a difficult divorce.
5	**6**
A mother tells her child's teacher not to let her child eat lunch because he was naughty at home and that is his punishment.	The parents of a 4-year-old boy are very concerned that he not get sick. They have asked that his teacher have him keep on his hooded fleece sweatshirt until the temperature reaches at least 70°. The child enjoys vigorous play. He often gets very sweaty.

Teaching the NAEYC Code of Ethical Conduct: A Resource Guide. Copyright © 2016 by NAEYC.

7	8
The teacher in the toddler classroom would like to move one of the children in her group to the 3-year-olds' room. She has not talked to the child's parents.	An experienced teacher thinks that her new colleague has used too many brightly colored commercial materials throughout her classroom. She is concerned that they will be very distracting for 3-year-olds.
9	**10**
A teacher is approached by the father of one of the children in her class. He asks her to testify on his behalf at an upcoming custody hearing.	The parents of a 3-year-old want his teachers to move him to the 4-year-olds' class. His teachers don't think he's ready.
11	**12**
The mother of a 6-month-old baby who is enrolled in a child care center wants to visit him during the school day to see what he is doing while he is away from home.	A very active 4-year-old enjoys eating lunch at school. He usually asks for seconds, and sometimes thirds. His mother asks that he be allowed just one serving at lunch, and that he be given a small afternoon snack. She says that she wants him to eat dinner with the family, but when he eats at school he is not hungry at dinnertime.

13

A teacher at a center that serves no sweets knows that families are asked to celebrate special occasions with fruit or vegetable plates. A mother who speaks little English brings a fancy cake to celebrate her son's birthday.

14

The father of a toddler comes to visit every day at lunch. The child screams and cries for an hour each time his daddy leaves.

15

A teacher is annoyed because the teacher in the room next door to hers knows only five songs and always sings them off-key.

16

A family asks the teacher in their child's classroom to help them find a child care subsidy.

17

A child's mother asks that her daughter not be allowed to play in the sandbox because she gets sand in her braids. Her teacher knows the benefits of sand play and doesn't want to exclude her.

18

A teacher is concerned because the ratio in her preschool room is 1:12, even though the school's brochure says this center maintains a 1:10 ratio for 3- and 4-year-olds.

A 1:12 ratio is permitted by licensing.

19

A father becomes very angry when he learns at pick-up time that his 2-year-old son was bitten just a few minutes before he had arrived. He demands that the teacher tell him who bit his son.

20

A teacher who teaches in a program that enrolls a number of Hmong children has noticed that the program does not translate any of its materials into the Hmong language.

21

A teacher who has carefully set the classroom up with well-equipped learning centers gets frustrated when children take blocks into the dramatic play center to be baked potatoes, baby bottles, and bananas.

22

A 3-year-old becomes very upset when his mother leaves in the morning. He kicks and cries loudly. The lead teacher punishes him by making him sit on a stool, sometimes for an hour or more. The assistant teacher believes discipline should be constructive and should show an understanding of what triggered the behavior. She wants to give him a safe outlet such as pounding clay or punching a pillow.

23

A coworker asks a teacher new to the center to join her in complaining about a coworker, saying, "We don't like to work with people like him." (He is of a different nationality than most of the staff.)

24

A reporter asks a teacher who works in a for-profit community program whether the school where he teaches supports a controversial piece of legislation involving young children.

What Kind of Issue Is It? Answer Sheet

1. **A child comes in with a hand-shaped bruise on his face.**

   » **Ethical Responsibility**

   The teacher has a responsibility to report suspected child abuse.

   P-1.1—Above all, we shall not harm children. We shall not participate in practices that are emotionally damaging, physically harmful, disrespectful, degrading, dangerous, exploitative, or intimidating to children. This principle has precedence over all others in this Code.

   P-1.9—When we have reasonable cause to suspect child abuse or neglect, we shall report it to the appropriate community agency.

2. **A teacher discovers a fruiting hot chili pepper growing in the play yard.**

   » **Ethical Responsibility**

   The teacher has a responsibility to remove the potentially harmful plant.

   P-1.11—When we become aware of a . . . situation that endangers the health, safety, or well-being of children, we have an ethical responsibility to protect children or inform parents and/or others who can.

3. **A teacher is required to administer a paper-and-pencil test to all the 4-year-olds in his class at the same time. Results will be used to place children in kindergarten.**

   » **Ethical Responsibility**

   The teacher has a responsibility to comply with regulations, but he may join advocacy efforts to change assessment practices that he believes can be damaging to children.

   P-3B.1—We shall follow all program policies. When we do not agree with program policies, we shall attempt to effect change.

   I-4.5—To work to ensure that appropriate assessment systems . . . are used for purposes that benefit children.

4. **A regular volunteer saw a 4-year-old having a difficult day. He was very aggressive and cried often. She asked the teacher what was going on. The teacher knows his parents are in the middle of a difficult divorce.**

   » **Ethical Responsibility**

   The teacher has a responsibility not to divulge anything she knows about the parents' personal issues.

Teaching the NAEYC Code of Ethical Conduct: A Resource Guide. Copyright © 2016 by NAEYC.

P-2.13—We shall maintain confidentiality and shall respect the family's right to privacy, refraining from disclosure of confidential information and intrusion into family life.

5. **A mother tells her child's teacher not to let her child eat lunch because he was naughty at home and that is his punishment.**

   » **Ethical Responsibility**

   The teacher must serve the child lunch.

   P-1.1—Above all, we shall not harm children. We shall not participate in practices that are emotionally damaging [or] physically harmful . . . to children. This principle has precedence over all others in this Code.

   I-1.4—To appreciate the vulnerability of children and their dependence on adults.

6. **The parents of a 4-year-old boy are very concerned that he not get sick. They have asked that his teacher have him keep on his hooded fleece sweatshirt until the temperature reaches at least 70°. The child enjoys vigorous play. He often gets very sweaty.**

   » **Ethical Dilemma**

   » **Responsibilities to Children**

   P-1.1—Above all, we shall not harm children. We shall not participate in practices that are emotionally damaging [or] physically harmful . . . to children. This principle has precedence over all others in this Code.

   I-1.5—To create and maintain safe and healthy settings that foster children's social [and] emotional . . . development and that respect their dignity and their contributions.

   » **Responsibilities to Families**

   I-2.2—To develop relationships of mutual trust and create partnerships with the families we serve.

   I-2.5—To respect the dignity and preferences of each family and to make an effort to learn about its structure, culture, . . . customs, and beliefs to ensure a culturally consistent environment for all children and families.

   I-2.6—To acknowledge families' childrearing values and their right to make decisions for their children.

   P-2.6—As families share information with us about their children and families, we shall ensure that families' input is an important contribution to the planning and implementation of the program.

7. **The teacher in the toddler classroom would like to move one of the children in her group to the 3-year-olds' room. She has not talked to the child's parents.**

    » **Ethical Responsibility**

    The teacher must discuss the child's placement with her parents and involve them in the decision to move their child to another classroom.

    P-1.4—We shall use two-way communications to involve all those with relevant knowledge (including families and staff) in decisions concerning a child, as appropriate, ensuring confidentiality of sensitive information.

    P-2.4—We shall ensure that the family is involved in significant decisions affecting their child.

8. **An experienced teacher thinks that her new colleague has used too many brightly colored commercial materials throughout her classroom. She is concerned that they will be very distracting for 3-year olds.**

    » **This Is Not an Ethical Issue.**

9. **A teacher is approached by the father of one of the children in her class. He asks her to testify on his behalf at an upcoming custody hearing.**

    » **Ethical Responsibility**

    The teacher cannot become an advocate for the father but can share factual information if asked to do so.

    P-2.14—In cases where family members are in conflict with one another, we shall work openly, sharing our observations of the child, to help all parties involved make informed decisions. We shall refrain from becoming an advocate for one party.

10. **The parents of a 3-year-old want his teachers to move him to the 4-year-olds' class. His teachers don't think he's ready.**

    » **Ethical Dilemma**

    » **Responsibilities to Children**

    I-1.2—To base program practices upon . . . particular knowledge of each child.

    I-1.3—To recognize and respect the unique qualities, abilities, and potential of each child.

    » **Responsibilities to Families**

    P-1.2—We shall care for and educate children in positive emotional and social environments that are cognitively stimulating.

    P-2.4—We shall ensure that the family is involved in significant decisions affecting their child.

Teaching the NAEYC Code of Ethical Conduct: A Resource Guide. Copyright © 2016 by NAEYC.

11. **The mother of a 6-month-old baby who is enrolled in a child care center wants to visit him during the school day to see what he is doing while he is away from home.**

   » **Ethical Responsibility**

   The baby's mother should be welcome to visit any time.

   P-2.1—We shall not deny family members access to their child's classroom or program setting unless access is denied by court order or other legal restriction.

12. **A very active 4-year-old enjoys eating lunch at school. He usually asks for seconds, and sometimes thirds. His mother asks that he be allowed just one serving at lunch, and that he be given a small afternoon snack. She says that she wants him to eat dinner with the family, but when he eats at school he is not hungry at dinnertime.**

   » **Ethical Dilemma**

   » **Responsibilities to Children**

   I-1.4—To appreciate the vulnerability of children and their dependence on adults.

   I-1.5—To create and maintain safe and healthy settings that foster children's social, emotional, cognitive, and physical development and that respect their dignity and their contributions.

   » **Responsibilities to Families**

   I-2.2—To develop relationships of mutual trust and create partnerships with the families we serve.

   I-2.4—To listen to families, acknowledge and build upon their strengths and competencies, and learn from families as we support them in their task of nurturing children.

   I-2.6—To acknowledge families' childrearing values and their right to make decisions for their children.

   P-2.6—As families share information with us about their children and families, we shall ensure that families' input is an important contribution to the planning and implementation of the program.

13. **A teacher at a center that serves no sweets knows that families are asked to celebrate special occasions with fruit or vegetable plates. A mother who speaks little English brings a fancy cake to celebrate her son's birthday.**

   » **Ethical Dilemma**

   » **Responsibility to Children**

   I-1.5—To create and maintain safe and healthy settings.

Teaching the NAEYC Code of Ethical Conduct: A Resource Guide. Copyright © 2016 by NAEYC.

» **Responsibilities to Families**

I-2.2—To develop relationships of mutual trust and create partnerships with the families we serve.

P-2.2—We shall inform families of program philosophy, policies, curriculum . . . and explain why we teach as we do.

P-2.5—We shall make every effort to communicate effectively with all families in a language that they understand.

14. **The father of a toddler comes to visit every day at lunch. The child screams and cries for an hour each time his daddy leaves.**

» **Ethical Dilemma**

» **Responsibilities to Children**

P-1.7—We shall strive to build individual relationships with each child; make individualized adaptations in teaching strategies, learning environments, and curricula; and consult with the family so that each child benefits from the program.

I-1.5—To create and maintain safe and healthy settings that foster children's social [and] emotional . . . development.

» **Responsibilities to Families**

P-2.1—We shall not deny family members access to their child's classroom or program setting.

15. **A teacher is annoyed because the teacher in the room next door sings just five songs and always sings them off-key.**

» **This is not an ethical issue.**

16. **A family asks the teacher in their child's classroom to help them find a child care subsidy.**

» **Ethical Responsibility**

The teacher should be knowledgeable about family supports such as child care vouchers, or should know where to find that information. She should provide this information to the family.

P-2.15—We shall be familiar with and appropriately refer families to community resources and professional support services. After a referral has been made, we shall follow up to ensure that services have been appropriately provided.

17. **A child's mother asks that her daughter not be allowed to play in the sandbox because she gets sand in her braids. Her teacher knows the benefits of sand play and doesn't want to exclude her.**

   » **Ethical Dilemma**

   » **Responsibilities to Children**

   I-1.2—To base program practices upon current knowledge and research in the field of early childhood education, child development, and related disciplines, as well as on particular knowledge of each child.

   I-1.5—To create and maintain safe and healthy settings that foster children's social, emotional, cognitive, and physical development.

   » **Responsibilities to Families**

   I-2.2—To develop relationships of mutual trust and create partnerships with the families we serve.

   I-2.6—To acknowledge families' childrearing values and their right to make decisions for their children.

18. **A teacher is concerned because the ratio in her preschool room is 1:12, even though the school's brochure says this center maintains a 1:10 ratio for 3- and 4-year-olds. A 1:12 ratio is permitted by licensing.**

   » **Ethical Responsibility**

   The teacher should talk with her director about the ratio in her room and urge her to either abide by the 1:10 ratio described in the brochure or to modify that description of her program.

   P-3B.1—We shall follow all program policies. When we do not agree with program policies, we shall attempt to effect change through constructive action within the organization.

   P-4.1—We shall communicate openly and truthfully about the nature and extent of services that we provide.

19. **A father becomes very angry when he learns at pick-up time that his 2-year-old son was bitten just a few minutes before he had arrived. He demands that the teacher tell him who bit his son.**

   » **Ethical Responsibility**

   The teacher must maintain confidentiality by never discussing one child's behavior with another child's family. She can assure the father that she is working with this child and the child's family to eliminate biting in the future.

   P-2.12—We shall develop written policies for the protection of confidentiality.

   P-2.13—We shall maintain confidentiality and shall respect the family's right to privacy, refraining from disclosure of confidential information.

20. **A teacher who teaches in a program that enrolls a number of Hmong children has noticed that the program does not translate any of its materials into the Hmong language.**

   » **Ethical Responsibility**

   Programs must make a good faith effort to communicate with all families in a language they understand. These efforts may include accessing community resources for translation services. There will be times, however, when translating materials into every families' home language will not be possible.

   P-2.5—We shall make every effort to communicate effectively with all families in a language that they understand. We shall use community resources for translation and interpretation when we do not have sufficient resources in our own programs.

21. **A teacher who has carefully set the classroom up with well-equipped learning centers gets frustrated when children take blocks into the dramatic play center to be baked potatoes, baby bottles, and bananas.**

   » **This Is Not an Ethical Issue.**

22. **A 3-year-old becomes very upset when his mother leaves in the morning. He kicks and cries loudly. The lead teacher punishes him by making him sit on a stool, sometimes for an hour or more. The assistant teacher believes discipline should be constructive and should show an understanding of what triggered the behavior. She wants to give him a safe outlet, such as pounding clay or punching a pillow.**

   » **Ethical Responsibility**

   The assistant teacher has a responsibility to talk with the lead teacher and share her concerns. It may be helpful for her to suggest some alternative approaches to guidance and discipline.

   I-1.2—To base program practices upon current knowledge and research in the field of early childhood education, child development, and related disciplines, as well as on particular knowledge of each child.

   P-3A.2—When we have concerns about the professional behavior of a coworker, we shall first let that person know of our concern in a way that shows respect for personal dignity and for the diversity to be found among staff members, and then attempt to resolve the matter collegially and in a confidential manner.

Teaching the NAEYC Code of Ethical Conduct: A Resource Guide. Copyright © 2016 by NAEYC.

23. **A coworker asks a teacher new to the center to join her in complaining about a coworker, saying, "We don't like to work with people like him." (He is of a different nationality than most of the staff.)**

» **Ethical Responsibility**

The new teacher must not participate in any discriminatory practices. She must decline to join those who are planning to complain.

P-3A.4—We shall not participate in practices that discriminate against a coworker because of sex, race, national origin, religious beliefs or other affiliations, age, marital status/family structure, disability, or sexual orientation.

24. **A reporter asks the teacher who works in a for-profit community program whether the school where he teaches supports a controversial piece of legislation involving young children.**

» **Ethical Responsibility**

He may express his personal opinion but must make it clear he is not speaking for the center, its owner, or its management.

P-3B.2—We shall speak or act on behalf of an organization only when authorized. We shall take care to acknowledge when we are speaking for the organization and when we are expressing a personal judgment.

Activity 5.3: Is This an Ethical Responsibility or an Ethical Dilemma?

Is This an Ethical Responsibility or an Ethical Dilemma?

Read each of these short scenarios. Refer to the definitions below and the NAEYC Code of Ethical Conduct to identify each as being either an **Ethical Responsibility** or an **Ethical Dilemma.** (Remember, an ethical issue must be either one or the other; it cannot be both.)

After you have identified an issue as being either a responsibility or a dilemma, list the items in the Code that should guide an ethical early childhood educator's response.

Ethical Responsibilities	Ethical Dilemmas
Ethical responsibilities are mandates describing what early childhood educators **must** or **must not** do. They describe how early childhood educators are required to act and are clearly spelled out in the Code.	Ethical dilemmas are situations that present conflicting obligations and have more than one possible resolution, each of which can be justified as being an ethical choice.

1. Frank is 19 months old. He likes to wrestle at home with his daddy. When he comes into the classroom, he tackles the babies and lays on them until his teacher comes to interest him in doing something else. *Is Frank's teacher facing an ethical responsibility or an ethical dilemma?*

Does Frank's teacher have an ethical responsibility?	If YES, list item(s) in the Code that indicate what his teacher **must** or **must not** do.
Is Frank's teacher facing an ethical dilemma?	If YES, list item(s) that identify his teacher's conflicting obligations.

Teaching the NAEYC Code of Ethical Conduct: A Resource Guide. Copyright © 2016 by NAEYC.

2. David is a 3-year-old boy who enjoys playing dress-up. His favorite outfits are the ones with lots of lace and ruffles. One day his father came early to pick him up and was very upset to see David wearing a princess costume. He told you that he did not want his son wearing girls' clothes. He asked you to either keep David out of the dramatic play center or remove the lacy and ruffled clothes you have there. You know the benefits of pretend play and have observed that all the children have been enjoying the fancy, brightly colored dress-up clothes you have for them to play with. *Are you facing an ethical responsibility or an ethical dilemma?*

Do you have an ethical responsibility?	If YES, list item(s) in the Code that indicate what you **must** or **must not** do.
Are you facing an ethical dilemma?	If YES, list item(s) that identify your conflicting obligations.

3. You have just started teaching in a large center and overhear some fellow teachers saying negative and critical things about colleagues as they relax in the teachers' lounge. You are uncomfortable. *Are you facing an ethical responsibility or an ethical dilemma?*

Do you have an ethical responsibility?	If YES, list item(s) in the Code that indicate what you **must** or **must not** do.
Are you facing an ethical dilemma?	If YES, list item(s) that identify your conflicting obligations.

4. For the past 30 years, the community preschool where Ms. Walker teaches has had a Mother's Day Breakfast prepared by the children and teachers. Families look forward to it! This year she has two families with two daddies. *Is Ms. Walker facing an ethical responsibility or an ethical dilemma?*

Does Ms. Walker have an ethical responsibility?	If YES, list item(s) in the Code that indicate what she **must** or **must not** do.
Is Ms. Walker facing an ethical dilemma?	If YES, list item(s) that identify her conflicting obligations.

5. You are concerned because your teaching assistant is spending too much time looking at her phone. It is not uncommon for her to text when she is supposed to be supervising children on the playground and to be reading and writing emails when she is supposed to be working with children during center time. You are not out of ratio, but you are not comfortable with the level of supervision she is providing. *Are you facing an ethical responsibility or an ethical dilemma?*

Do you have an ethical responsibility?	If YES, list item(s) in the Code that indicate what you **must** or **must not** do.
Are you facing an ethical dilemma?	If YES, list item(s) that identify your conflicting obligations.

Teaching the NAEYC Code of Ethical Conduct: A Resource Guide. Copyright © 2016 by NAEYC.

Is This an Ethical Responsibility
or an Ethical Dilemma Answer Sheet

1. Frank is 19 months old. He likes to wrestle at home with his daddy. When he comes into the classroom, he tackles the babies and lays on them until his teacher comes to interest him in doing something else.

    Frank's teacher has an **ethical responsibility**. He must ensure the babies' safety.

    These items in the Code describe relevant ethical responsibilities to children:

    *   **P-1.1**–Above all, we shall not harm children. We shall not participate in practices that are emotionally damaging [or] physically harmful . . . to children. *This principle has precedence over all others in this Code.*

    *   **P-1.11**—When we become aware of a practice or situation that endangers the health, safety, or well-being of children, we have an ethical responsibility to protect children or inform parents and/or others who can.

2. David is a 3-year-old boy who enjoys playing dress-up. His favorite outfits are the ones with lots of lace and ruffles. One day his father came early to pick him up and was very upset to see David wearing a princess costume. He told you that he did not want his son wearing girls' clothes. He asked you to either keep David out of the dramatic play center or remove the lacy and ruffled clothes you have there. You know the benefits of pretend play and have observed that all the children have been enjoying the fancy, brightly colored dress-up clothes you have for them to play with.

    You are facing an **ethical dilemma**. You have to balance your knowledge of child development and the contributions of dress-up play with your responsibilities to honor families' requests.

    These items in the Code describe relevant ethical responsibilities to children:

    *   **I-1.2**—To base program practices upon current knowledge and research in the field of early childhood education, child development, and related disciplines, as well as on particular knowledge of each child.

    *   **I-1.5**—To create and maintain safe and healthy settings that foster children's social [and] emotional . . . development and that respect their dignity and their contributions.

    These items in the Code describe relevant ethical responsibilities to families:

    *   **I-2.2**—To develop relationships of mutual trust and create partnerships with the families we serve.

    *   **I-2.5**—To respect the dignity and preferences of each family . . . .

Teaching the NAEYC Code of Ethical Conduct: A Resource Guide. Copyright © 2016 by NAEYC.

- **I-2.6**—To acknowledge families' childrearing values and their right to make decisions for their children.
- **P-2.6**—As families share information with us about their children and families, we shall ensure that families' input is an important contribution to the planning and implementation of the program.

3. You have just begun to teach in a large center and overhear some fellow teachers saying negative and critical things about colleagues as they relax in the teachers' lounge. You are uncomfortable.

   You are facing an **ethical dilemma**. You have to balance your responsibilities to maintain a respectful school environment with your responsibilities to maintain cooperative relationships with colleagues.

   These items in the Code describe relevant ethical responsibilities to colleagues:
   - **I-3A.1**—To establish and maintain relationships of respect, trust, confidentiality, collaboration, and cooperation with coworkers.
   - **P-3A.2**—When we have concerns about the professional behavior of a coworker, we shall first let that person know of our concern in a way that shows respect for personal dignity and for the diversity to be found among staff members, and then attempt to resolve the matter collegially and in a confidential manner.
   - **P-3B.4**—If we have concerns about a colleague's behavior, and children's well-being is not at risk, we may address the concern with that individual.

4. For the past 30 years, the community preschool where Ms. Walker teaches has had a Mother's Day Breakfast made by the children and teachers. Families look forward to it! This year she has two families with two daddies.

   Ms. Walker has an **ethical responsibility**. She must respect all children's family structure.

   These items in the Code describe relevant ethical responsibilities to children:
   - **I-1.10**—To ensure that each child's culture, language, ethnicity, and family structure are recognized and valued in the program.
   - **P-1.2**—We shall care for and educate children in positive emotional and social environments . . . that support each child's culture, language, ethnicity, and family structure.
   - **P-1.3**—We shall not participate in practices that discriminate against children by . . . excluding them from programs or activities on the basis of . . . the marital status/family structure, [or] sexual orientation . . . of their families.

Teaching the NAEYC Code of Ethical Conduct: A Resource Guide. Copyright © 2016 by NAEYC.

5. You are concerned because your teaching assistant is spending too much time looking at her phone. It is not uncommon for her to text when she is supposed to be supervising children on the playground and to be reading and writing email when she is supposed to be supervising children during center time. You are not out of ratio, but you are not comfortable with the level of supervision she is providing.

You are facing an **ethical responsibility**. You must ensure that the children in your care are always adequately supervised.

These items in the Code describe ethical responsibilities to children, to coworkers, and to the program.

- **P-1.1**–Above all, we shall not harm children. We shall not participate in practices that are . . . physically harmful . . . to children. This principle has precedence over all others in this Code.

- **P-1.11**—When we become aware of a practice or situation that endangers the health, safety, or well-being of children, we have an ethical responsibility to protect children or inform parents and/or others who can.

- **P-3A.2**—When we have concerns about the professional behavior of a coworker, we shall first let that person know of our concern in a way that shows respect for personal dignity . . . and then attempt to resolve the matter collegially and in a confidential manner.

- **I-3B.1**—To assist the program in providing the highest quality of service.

Selected Cases

We have been collecting cases that involve ethical issues in early childhood education since work began on the development of the NAEYC Code in the l980s, and we have continued to add new cases throughout the years. Some of the cases in this collection are based on our own experiences; others come from the first ethics survey published in *Young Children* (Feeney & Kipnis 1985), from the cases in *Ethics and the Early Childhood Educator* and the Focus on Ethics column published in *Young Children*, from the Australian early childhood ethics publications *Getting Ethical: A Resource Book for Workshop Leaders* (Fasoli & Woodrow 1991) and *Will My Response Be Ethical?* (Newman & Pollnitz 2001), and from our college students and early childhood educators who have attended our workshops and conference presentations. All of the cases in this book are based on real situations. We believe they are a good cross-section of the kinds of ethical issues likely to be encountered by those with whom you work.

When you use cases in your courses or workshops, it's important to select those that reflect issues that are most relevant for your group or contain content you particularly want to highlight. You might embellish them by adding the names of fictitious centers, schools, and individuals to reflect the identity of your community.

We have organized this collection of cases by sections of the NAEYC Code. They are numbered to indicate the section of the Code and the number of the case within that section (for example, Case 2.11. refers to the 11th case within "Section 2: Ethical Responsibilities to Families"). Cases are presented in an easy-to-copy format so you can duplicate them to use in a workshop, conference, or class session.

Most of these cases are **ethical dilemmas** (situations that present conflicting obligations and have more than one justifiable resolution); some are **ethical responsibilities** (situations where the Code states what early childhood educators **must** or **must not** do). When dealing with a dilemma, students should identify the stakeholders, the conflicting obligations, and the relevant sections of the Code. When the card is marked **R** for responsibility, students should identify the items in the Code that spell out the early childhood educator's responsibility.

Case Cards—Keyed to the 4 Sections of the NAEYC Code

Section I: Ethical responsibilities to children

Case cards 1.1 to 1.5: Most often situations that focus on children involve their welfare and require early childhood educators to balance the needs of an individual child against their responsibilities to the entire group.

Section II: Ethical responsibilities to families

Case cards 2.1 to 2.12: The ethical issues most frequently reported by early childhood educators concern relationships with families. Most of the situations involve obligations to the child and to family members that are in conflict. Other issues have to do with confidentiality, divorce and custody, and situations in which families and early childhood educators have different ideas about educational priorities.

Section III: Ethical responsibilities to colleagues, employers, and employees

Case cards 3.1 to 3.15: Ethical issues involving colleagues are frequently reported by early childhood educators. These tend to involve professional behavior, program practices, and program management.

Section IV: Ethical responsibilities to community and society

Case cards 4.1 to 4.7: Teachers' concerns about suspected child abuse fit into this category, as do violations of regulations designed to protect children and situations that lead early childhood educators to be concerned about the welfare of children. In recent years concerns about inappropriate assessment of young children have been included in this category.

Teaching the NAEYC Code of Ethical Conduct: A Resource Guide. Copyright © 2016 by NAEYC.

1.1 A large and extremely aggressive 4-year-old boy in your class is frightening and hurting other children. Your director and a mental health specialist have been unable to help. His parents feel that his behavior is typical for boys his age; they won't get counseling. You and your coteacher are becoming stressed and tired, and you are worried that the other children are not getting the attention they need.

1.2 A 3-year-old in your class spends most of her time rolling a truck alongside the block area. She howls and disrupts large group activities and bangs her head to put herself to sleep at naptime. Her pediatrician has told her parents, "She will grow out of it." You've found she needs constant one-on-one attention, and other children's parents are beginning to complain that this child takes too much of the teachers' time and energy.

1.3 You are a kindergarten teacher. A student's mother comes to pick up her child and drive him home. From her slurred speech and clumsy movements, you suspect that she has been drinking heavily.

Variation: The mother arrives by bus and plans to take the child home on the bus.

1.4 You have successfully taught first grade in a predominantly Hispanic neighborhood for several years, and your efforts to understand the culture are appreciated. One day a father with whom you have a particularly good relationship remarks in a parent meeting that he regularly swats his child with a belt to keep him in line and teach him respect. Soon after hearing this remark, you see marks on the child's back and legs that could have been left by a belt. You realize there are cultural differences about appropriate discipline for young children and are troubled by what appears to be abuse.

R

R

1.5 You are a preschool teacher. On one occasion you find yourself seated next to a pediatrician who is a well-known expert on child abuse. You realize that this presents a great opportunity, and you ask for information that might help you decide what to do about a child in your group whom you suspect is being physically abused. The doctor gives you some general advice but says that he needs to know more about the situation to give you better guidance.

2.1 The mother of a 4-year-old in your class has asked that he not nap at school, because when he naps he stays up too late at night, making it difficult for her to get up at 5 a.m. to go to work. You have observed that he needs his nap to stay in good spirits in the afternoon.

Teaching the NAEYC Code of Ethical Conduct: A Resource Guide. Copyright © 2016 by NAEYC.

2.2 A parent calls you, the center director, to express concern that her 3-year-old daughter is permitted to walk the short distance to the bathroom without an adult accompanying her and waiting. You reassure her that the security in your center is good, but she insists that her child must be individually escorted to the bathroom.

2.3 A father informs you, the center director, that his daughter who has chronic asthma needs to stay indoors every time he suspects she may be becoming ill. At first you arrange for a floater to stay with her, but your center's enrollment has increased and assigning a staff member to supervise one child has become impossible. The parent feels that the school should be able to provide services to children like his who have chronic health problems.

2.4 Your center serves snack and lunch. A 3-year-old is always asking for food, and the child's parent feels the child should always be given food when she asks for it. The parent says that you are abusing the child when you do not provide food whenever she wants it.

2.5 You are a new graduate who has accepted a position teaching kindergarten at a rural school in a community in which many families have low incomes and where students' test scores are very low. You have set up learning centers, and things are going well. You are shocked when your principal tells you the students' parents are adamant that they don't want children to "just play." They expect children to complete workbook pages at school and also expect their children to have workbook pages for homework.

2.6 A father comes to see you, complaining that his 4-year-old son has been allowed to wear a dress in school. He tells you that you he does not want his son to *ever* dress up like a girl.

2.7 The parent of a child in your group of 3-year-olds has asked you not to let her daughter participate in any art or sensory activities that may be messy or dirty. She doesn't have enough time at night to bathe the child and clean her clothes. And since it is so difficult to remove the paint, glue, dirt, and other stains the child brings home, she needs to replace the child's school clothing frequently.

2.8 You are a teacher in a kindergarten class that includes several children with special needs. You are uncomfortable when parents ask questions about children in your class, and you don't know how to respond when they ask, "What's wrong with him?" or "Why does he behave like that?" or "How do you handle her slowness?"

R

2.9 A parent of a kindergartner has told you that the family follows a strict vegetarian regimen for spiritual and health reasons. This parent says that her son has no interest in meat or fish, and he should not be encouraged to eat these foods. The child becomes quite interested in other children's lunches. One day you find the child taking a bite from his friend's ham sandwich. The child begs you not to tell his parents because he would be punished. He says he didn't like the ham and was sorry he had tried it. You think no harm has been done and don't tell the family about the incident. Two weeks later you see the child and his buddy quietly swap sandwiches—cheese for chicken!

2.10 A classmate bites a 20-month-old boy in your group in an altercation over a toy. You apply ice and comfort him and write a report of the incident for the school files. When the mother picks him up, she is informed that her son was bitten during play, that the skin was not broken, and that ice was applied. The mother is angry about what happened. "Who bit him?" she demands.

R

2.11 You are the director of a program that is committed to serving healthy foods. Your center doesn't regularly serve cookies, cakes, or other foods full of sugar, fats, or preservatives. The program's family handbook describes these policies. It states clearly that birthday cakes are not allowed. One morning a mother who is new to the center, who has been shy about participating and whose mastery of English is limited, arrives with a large, elaborately decorated cake to celebrate her daughter's birthday.

2.12 The aggression of a 4-year-old in your class is a challenge. His outbursts have become more frequent and he has injured a classmate. You have discussed the issue with his parents and have been developing a plan to help him control his emotions. Recently the mother stopped by your classroom and reminded you how important it is to their family that the child behaves well in school. She asked you to report to her whenever he misbehaves so they can punish him. You are concerned based on your observations of the parent's interactions with the child. You suspect that this family's approach to discipline is quite harsh.

3.1 You are a preschool director. One day you go to a classroom to give a teacher a message at naptime and observe two teachers discussing the home life of a child whose father has been arrested for drunk driving.

Teaching the NAEYC Code of Ethical Conduct: A Resource Guide. Copyright © 2016 by NAEYC.

3.2 Your coteacher is often angry about administrative decisions made in the center. On a number of occasions, you have heard her complaining about these things to parents.

3.3 A 4-year-old in your group who is usually happy and cooperative has been irritable. He plays by himself, seldom smiles or laughs, and frequently quarrels with the other children. You mention the change in his behavior to his mother. She tells you that she and her husband have been arguing a great deal and have decided to get a divorce. So far they have told no one. A few days later, you are working with a volunteer when the child spills paint on the floor. She asks the child to help her clean it up, but he refuses. (continues on the next card)

3.3 (continued) She asks him a second time, gently but firmly, and he shouts that he will not. He starts screaming and knocks over two cans of paint. It takes half an hour to calm him. Later, you and the volunteer sit down for coffee. She is still upset at the child's behavior and asks if you know why his behavior has changed so drastically.

3.4 You are a teacher in a Christian preschool and also a member of the sponsoring church. All preschool employees are required to sign a contract agreeing to follow high standards of moral behavior. You like and respect the teacher who works in the classroom next to yours, and the two of you sometimes talk about your private lives. She is a single parent. One day she tells you that she works as a topless dancer in a nearby nightclub to help support her child. She asks you not to tell the director or the board, who would fire her for breach of contract.

3.5 You are a preschool director who hears through the grapevine that a former employee of yours, whose work was always acceptable, was charged with abusing her own child but was acquitted. You receive a call from another director who says that she is considering hiring your former employee, who has given your name as a reference.

3.6 You have been informed that a 2-year-old in the next classroom has been diagnosed with contagious diarrhea. You expect that the families will be alerted to the illness through a posted notice, but the director of your center has dismissed the problem. She tells teachers to be sure to wear gloves and wash their hands after changing the child. You go to the director and express your concern. The director says she doesn't want to upset the parents and that good hygiene should take care of the problem.

R

Teaching the NAEYC Code of Ethical Conduct: A Resource Guide. Copyright © 2016 by NAEYC.

3.7 You and your coteacher work with a group of twenty 4-year-olds (two of whom have special needs). Your classroom is a portable building, one of six units clustered around a small, central courtyard. Several times recently your coteacher has left the classroom for periods of up to 30 minutes to conduct personal business.

3.8 You have recently begun a new job teaching in a community preschool. One afternoon in the lounge you hear a coworker make an insulting joke about children and families of a particular ethnic group. It makes you feel uncomfortable, and you think her comments show an unhealthy prejudice; however, everyone else laughs.

3.9 You are a preschool teacher. The teacher in the class next door is not doing a great job. She often comes to school without having made any lesson plans and borrows activities from you. Her classroom is chaotic, and you have seen children doing things you think are inappropriate, even dangerous.

3.10 You are a teacher in a toddler group. A colleague tells you that she met the new preschool teacher and is "pretty sure" that he is gay. While she knows that professional conduct has nothing to do with sexual orientation, she says she is uncomfortable having him in a classroom. She asks you to go to the director with her to voice this concern.

3.11 You teach in a public school kindergarten. You are on good terms with the other teachers but feel they do not completely accept you because you are young and enthusiastic about teaching. The first grade teacher in the classroom next to yours has the reputation of being a strict disciplinarian. You go into her room one day to borrow some paper, and you see her hit a child.

R

3.12 You have just graduated from an early childhood education program where you learned about developmentally appropriate practice and the value of play. You take a job working in a child care center near your home and are delighted that it pays well. You are surprised to find that you are expected to have the 3- and 4-year-olds in your class sit for long hours each day and do worksheets. When you question this approach, you are told that this is how they have always taught, and teachers and families are very happy with it.

3.13 You are an experienced teacher with a degree in early childhood education. Your 4-year-old daughter attends the school where you teach. She has been placed in the class taught by a new teacher who used to teach in an elementary school. You are concerned about the worksheets she is bringing home each day. You go to the director to register your objection, both as a parent and as a staff member. You see a workbook that your daughter's teacher has left in the office—it is meant for grade 2! The director sympathizes with your concern and tells you she will discuss it with the teacher next week. Three weeks later, the flow of worksheets continues.

3.14 You are a kindergarten teacher in an inner-city elementary school. All the children in your school are required to take the Metropolitan Readiness Test during the first week of kindergarten. The three-day test is administered solely to determine qualifications for federal funding. You think that it is an ordeal for the children that is both frustrating and demeaning. You protest, but the administration insists that you give the children the test.

3.15 You are a second-year teacher who works with 3- and 4-year-olds in a private preschool program. You have been assigned to coteach with a teacher who has more than 20 years of experience. The arrangement is okay for a few months, but then you start to have reservations. Your coteacher is using materials that are dated and not developmentally appropriate. She is also quite impatient with the children, and she spends quite a bit of time on her phone texting and reading email. (continues on the next card)

3.15 (continued) You try to talk to your coteacher about your concerns, but it does not help the situation. After you talk with her, she begins to gossip about you and post unfavorable comments about you on Facebook. You try talking to the director, but she tells you that she has faith in the coteacher, and she is sure that the two of you can work it out.

You are increasingly stressed and unhappy about the situation. You are thinking about quitting and finding a job in a more congenial program, but you do not want to leave the children.

4.1 You are the director of a child care center. A child in your center shows definite signs of being abused. You know that you should report the case to your local child protective services agency, but the last time you referred a child to them a worker visited the family but did not promptly intervene. The family left town, never to be heard from again.

4.2 You are a preschool teacher who has just moved to another state and taken a job. You have always included lots of cooking in your curriculum and believe that it is a great way to motivate children and integrate learning. After your first cooking project, the director of your new school takes you aside and tells you that cooking is against licensing regulations in this state because of potential health and safety risks to children.

R

Teaching the NAEYC Code of Ethical Conduct: A Resource Guide. Copyright © 2016 by NAEYC.

4.3 A number of families have recently moved their children to your center from another one in your neighborhood. They have told you stories of what happened to their children in that center. They describe it as being dirty, crowded, and possibly dangerous. One day on your way to work, you drive by to check it out for yourself. You see an open lot covered with asphalt and dry grass. There are a few rusting pieces of playground equipment. Several children are looking through a chain link fence. There are no adults in sight.

4.4 You are a center director. The teachers in your school have high heels for children to wear in the dress-up corner. The children enjoy them, and they seem to encourage elaborate make-believe play. You recently heard that your new licensing worker has been telling directors at other centers that they must get rid of high heels because these could be used by children as weapons. You learn that this inspector will be coming to your school next week for your annual inspection.

4.5 You are the director of a preschool that serves families with low incomes. Your rent is very low, which allows you to charge a low tuition to families. Your landlord has let the building fall into dangerous disrepair. There are no other low-rent facilities in your community that could house a preschool.

4.6 You are a teacher in a child development center that is out of compliance with numerous state licensing regulations. Violations include playground equipment that needs to be repaired, infrequent fire drills, rooms filled beyond their licensed capacity, and failure to maintain required adult–child ratios. You are aware that the director sometimes gives incomplete or misleading information about these things to state licensing inspectors. You know that it isn't right to mislead the inspectors, but you are afraid to do anything that would jeopardize your employment.

4.7 You are a kindergarten teacher at a public school in a community where most families have low incomes. Third grade reading scores at your school have dropped dramatically in the last few years. The state and district offices of education have placed pressure the school's administrators to raise third grade reading scores. In order to get children ready for higher academic expectations and the mandated third grade test, district administrators have decided that teachers will administer a standardized test of reading and math achievement to all kindergarten children in the district to demonstrate that they are making progress toward reaching the district's goals. (continues on the next card)

R

4.7 (continued) You pride yourself on providing many meaningful, hands-on learning experiences and you do not think that a paper and pencil test is appropriate for kindergartners. You know that the test-taking experience will be stressful for the children in your class, you also understand your obligation to follow the district mandate.

R

Glossary of Terms

Code of ethics. Defines the core values of the field and provides guidance for what professionals should do when they encounter conflicting obligations or responsibilities in their work.

Core values. Commitments held by a profession that are consciously and knowingly embraced by its practitioners because they make a contribution to society. There is a difference between personal values and the core values of a profession.

Ethical commitment. Intention to apply learning about ethical responsibilities and ethical analysis in the workplace.

Ethical deliberation. Careful thought or discussion of ethical issues in order to make a decision.

Ethical dilemma. A moral conflict that involves determining appropriate conduct when an individual faces conflicting professional values and responsibilities. (A dilemma has two defensible resolutions.)

Ethical issues. Situations that involve determining what is right and wrong, and what rights and responsibilities and issues of human welfare are part of the situation.

Ethical judgment. (Terms with a similar meaning are *moral judgment, ethical decision making,* and *ethical analysis.*) The ability to make moral distinctions, understand moral concepts, and engage in increasingly higher levels of moral reasoning.

Ethical responsibilities. (Also referred to as *professional responsibilities.*) Behaviors that one must or must not engage in. Ethical responsibilities are clear-cut and are spelled out in the Code of Ethical Conduct.

Ethics. The study of right and wrong, or duty and obligation, that involves critical reflection on morality and the ability to make choices between values and the examination of the moral dimensions of relationships.

Moral behavior. Behaving in ways that reflect standards of morality.

Moral development. The emergence and change in moral understanding from infancy through adulthood. Increasing ability over time to distinguish right from wrong.

Moral development stages. A set of stages regarding conceptions of right and wrong that begin in childhood and become more advanced as individuals move into adulthood. The progression through these stages is a result of intellectual ability, increased maturity, and experience.

Moral reasoning. The ability to understand moral concepts and to engage in increasingly higher levels of moral reflection; deliberation by which an individual determines alternatives that are morally right and morally wrong.

Morality. People's views of what is good, right, and proper; their beliefs about their obligations; and their ideas about how they should behave.

Professional ethics. The moral commitments of a profession that involve moral reflection that extends and enhances the personal morality practitioners bring to their work, that concern actions of right and wrong in the workplace, and that help individuals resolve moral dilemmas they encounter in their work.

Values. Qualities or principles that individuals believe to be desirable or worthwhile and that they prize for themselves, for others, and for the world in which they live.

Sources for glossary definitions:

Kidder, R.M. 2009. *How Good People Make Tough Choices: Resolving the Dilemmas of Ethical Living*. Rev. ed. New York: Harper.

NAEYC. 2011. *Code of Ethical Conduct and Statement of Commitment*. Washington, DC: NAEYC.

Rest, J.R. 1986. *Moral Development: Advances in Research and Theory*. New York: Praeger.

Richardson, H.S. 2014. "Moral Reasoning." Winter Edition, *The Stanford Encyclopedia of Philosophy*. Stanford, CA: Metaphysics Research Lab, Center for the Study of Language and Information, Stanford University. http://plato.stanford.edu/archives/win2014/entries/reasoning-moral.

References and Resources

Armon, C. 1998. "Adult Moral Development, Experience, and Education." *Journal of Moral Education* 27 (3): 345–70.

Bebeau, M.J. 1993. "Designing an Outcome-Based Ethics Curriculum for Professional Education: Strategies and Evidence of Effectiveness." *Journal of Moral Education* 22 (3): 313–26.

Bebeau, M.J. 1994. "Influencing the Moral Dimensions of Dental Practice." Chapt. 7 in *Moral Development in the Professions: Psychology and Applied Ethics*, eds. J.R. Rest & D. Narváez, 121–46. Hillsdale, NJ: Erlbaum.

Bebeau, M.J., & S.J. Thoma. 1994. "The Impact of a Dental Ethics Curriculum on Moral Reasoning." *Journal of Dental Education* 58 (9): 684–92.

Brendel, J.M., J.B. Kolbert, & V.A. Foster. 2002. "Promoting Student Cognitive Development." *Journal of Adult Development* 9 (3): 217–27.

Brophy-Herb, H.E., M.J. Kostelnik, & L.C. Stein. 2001. "A Developmental Approach to Teaching About Ethics Using the NAEYC Code of Ethical Conduct." *Young Children* 56 (1): 80–84.

CAEP. 2014. *Standards for Advanced Programs*. Washington, DC: CAEP. https://caepnet.files.wordpress.com/2014/08/caep_standards_for_advanced_programs1.pdf.

Campbell, E. 2013. "Cultivating Moral and Ethical Professional Practice: Interdisciplinary Lessons and Teacher Education." Chapt. 3 in *The Moral Work of Teaching and Teacher Education: Preparing and Supporting Practitioners*, eds. M.N. Sanger & R.D. Osguthorpe, 29–43. New York: Teachers College Press.

Copple, C., & S. Bredekamp, eds. 2009. *Developmentally Appropriate Practice in Early Childhood Programs Serving Children From Birth to Age 8*. 3rd ed. Washington, DC: NAEYC.

Council for the Accreditation of Educator Preparation (CAEP). 2013. *Accreditation Standards*. Washington, DC: CAEP. http://caepnet.org/standards/introduction.

Daneker, D. 2007. "Developing Ethical Reasoning Ability Using an Applied Ethics Course." *American Counseling Association Vistas Online.* https://www.counseling.org/resources/library/vistas/2007-V-online-MSWord-files/Daneker2.pdf.

Fasoli, L., & C. Woodrow. 1991. *Getting Ethical: A Resource Book for Workshop Leaders. Australian Early Childhood Education Resource Booklets No. 3*. Watson, Australian Capital Territory: Australian Early Childhood Association.

Feeney, S., & N.K. Freeman. 1999/2005. *Ethics and the Early Childhood Educator: Using the NAEYC Code.* 1st ed. Washington, DC: NAEYC.

Feeney, S., N.K. Freeman, & P.J. Pizzolongo. 2012. *Ethics and the Early Childhood Educator: Using the NAEYC Code.* 2nd ed. Washington, DC: NAEYC.

Feeney, S., & N.K. Freeman. 2013. "The Birthday Cake: Balancing Responsibilities to Children and Families." *Young Children* 68 (3): 96–99.

Feeney, S., & K. Kipnis. 1985. "Public Policy Report and Survey. Professional Ethics in Early Childhood Education." *Young Children* 40 (3): 54–58.

Freeman, N.K., & M.H. Brown. 1996. "Ethics Instruction for Preservice Teachers: How Are We Doing in ECE?" *Journal of Early Childhood Teacher Education* 17 (2): 5–18.

Freeman, N.K., & S. Feeney. 2006. "The New Face of Early Care and Education: Who Are We? Where Are We Going?" Viewpoint. *Young Children* 61 (5): 10–16.

Freeman, N.K., & S. Feeney. 2009. "Professionalism and Ethics in Early Care and Education." Chapt. 9 in *Continuing Issues in Early Childhood Education,* 3rd ed., eds. S. Feeney, A. Galper, & C. Seefeldt, 196–211. Upper Saddle River, NJ: Merrill/Pearson.

Freeman, N.K., & S. Feeney. 2016. "What Teachers Need to Know: Professional Ethics." Chapt. 10 in *Handbook of Early Childhood Teacher Education,* eds. L.J. Couse & S.L. Recchia, 148–62. New York: Routlege.

Gilligan, C. [1982] 1993. *In a Different Voice: Psychological Theory and Women's Development.* Cambridge, MA: Harvard University Press.

Hostetler, K.D. 1997. *Ethical Judgement in Teaching.* Boston: Allyn & Bacon.

Johnson, L.E., J.W. Vare, & R.B. Evers. 2013. "Let the Theory Be Your Guide: Addressing the Moral Work of Teaching." Chapt. 7 in *The Moral Work of Teaching and Teacher Education: Preparing and Supporting Practitioners,* eds. M.N. Sanger & R.D. Osguthorpe, 92–114. New York: Teachers College Press.

Katz, L.G. 1995. "The Developmental Stages of Teachers." Chapt. 12 in *Talks With Teachers of Young Children: A Collection,* 203–210. Norwood, NJ: Ablex.

Keefer, M.W., S.E. Wilson, H. Dankowicz, & M.C. Loui. 2014. "The Importance of Formative Assessment in Science and Engineering Ethics Education: Some Evidence and Practical Advice." *Science and Engineering Ethics* 20 (1): 249–60.

Kidder, R.M. 2009. *How Good People Make Tough Choices: Resolving the Dilemmas of Ethical Living.* Rev. ed. New York: Harper.

Kipnis, K. 1987. "How to Discuss Professional Ethics." *Young Children* 42 (4): 26–30.

Kohlberg, L., & R.H. Hersh. 1977. "Moral Development: A Review of the Theory." *Theory Into Practice* 16 (2): 53–59.

Levine, F.J. & J.L. Tapp. 1977. "The Dialectic of Legal Socialization in Community and School." Chapt. 15 in *Law, Justice, and the Individual in Society: Psychological and Legal Issues,* eds. J.L. Tapp, & F.J. Levine, 163–82. New York: Holt, Rinehart, & Winston.

NAEYC, NAECTE (National Association of Early Childhood Teacher Educators), & ACCESS (American Associate Degree Early Childhood Teacher Educators). 2004. "Code of Ethical Conduct: Supplement for Early Childhood Adult Educators." Joint position statement supplement. Washington, DC: NAEYC.

NAEYC. 2006. "Code of Ethical Conduct: Supplement for Program Administrators." Position statement supplement. Washington, DC: NAEYC.

NAEYC. 2011. "Code of Ethical Conduct and Statement of Commitment." Position statement. Washington, DC: NAEYC. www.naeyc.org/positionstatements/ethical_conduct.

NAEYC. 2012. "2010 NAEYC Standards for Initial and Advanced Early Childhood Professional Preparation Programs." Washington, DC: NAEYC. www.naeyc.org/caep/files/caep/NAEYC%20Initial%20and%20Advanced%20Standards%2010_2012.pdf.

NAEYC. 2015. "NAEYC Early Childhood Program Accreditation Criteria and Guidance for Assessment." https://www.naeyc.org/academy/files/academy/Standards%20and%20Accreditation%20Criteria%20%26%20Guidance%20for%20Assessment_10.2015_0.pdf.

Newman, L., & L. Pollnitz. 2001. *Will My Response Be Ethical? A Reflective Process to Guide the Practice of Early Childhood Students and Professionals*. Multimedia kit. Melbourne: Video Education Australia.

Nolte, S. 1998. *PACE (Professional and Career Education for Early Childhood) Training Manual for ED 140*. Rev. ed. Honolulu: Honolulu Community College.

Rest, J.R. 1986. *Moral Development: Advances in Research and Theory*. New York: Praeger.

Richardson, H.S. 2014. "Moral Reasoning." *The Stanford Encyclopedia of Philosophy*. Stanford, CA: Metaphysics Research Lab, Center for the Study of Language and Information, Stanford University. http://plato.stanford.edu/archives/win2014/entries/reasoning-moral.

Sanger, M.N., & R.D. Osguthorpe, eds. 2013. *The Moral Work of Teaching and Teacher Education: Preparing and Supporting Practitioners*. New York: Teachers College Press.

Sanger, M.N., R.D. Osguthorpe, & G.D. Fenstermacher. 2013. "The Moral Work of Teaching in Teacher Education." Chapt. 1 in *The Moral Work of Teaching and Teacher Education: Preparing and Supporting Practitioners,* eds. M.N Sanger & R.D. Osguthorpe, 3–13. New York: Teachers College Press.

Torres de Freitas, S.F., D.F. Kovaleski, A.F. Boing, & W. Ferreira de Olveira. 2006. "Stages of Moral Development Among Brazilian Dental Students." *Journal of Dental Education* 70 (3): 296–306.

Warnick, B.R., & S.K. Silverman. 2011. "A Framework for Professional Ethics Courses in Teacher Education." *Journal of Teacher Education* 62 (3): 273–85.

About the Authors

Stephanie Feeney, PhD, is professor emerita of education at the University of Hawaii at Mānoa, where she taught undergraduate and graduate courses in early childhood and elementary education and directed the master's program in early childhood education. She received her bachelor's degree at UCLA, master's degree at Harvard University, and PhD at Claremont Graduate University.

Professor Feeney has been involved in early childhood policy formation in Hawaii and nationally for many years. She has served on the governing boards of NAEYC and the National Association for Early Childhood Teacher Educators (NAECTE).

She is co-author of the original NAEYC Code of Ethical Conduct and Statement of Commitment, and has participated in all of the revisions of the Code as well as development of the supplements to the Code for adult educators and program administrators. She is co-author of *Ethics and the Early Childhood Educator* and co-author of the Focus on Ethics column that is a regular feature of NAEYC's journal, *Young Children*.

Professor Feeney has written and lectured extensively on ethics and professionalism in early childhood education. She is author of numerous articles and books, including *Professionalism in Early Childhood Education: Doing Our Best for Young Children* and *Early Childhood Education in Asia and the Pacific*. She is co-author of *Who Am I in the Lives of Children?* (now in its 10th edition) and *Continuing Issues in Early Childhood Education* (third edition).

Nancy K. Freeman, PhD, is professor emerita of education at the University of South Carolina in Columbia, where she was a member of the early childhood faculty. She taught graduate and undergraduate courses in early childhood education and did extensive work to support the professional development of the early care and education workforce, particularly those who work with infants and toddlers.

She received her bachelor's degree from St. Mary's College, Notre Dame, Indiana, and graduated from the master's and PhD programs at the University of South Carolina.

Professor Freeman chaired the South Carolina Governor's Advisory Committee on the Regulation of Child Care for many years, and has provided leadership to a wide variety of the state's early childhood initiatives. She was the president of the National Association of Early Childhood Teacher Educators (NAECTE) and has held many positions on its board.

She has written and lectured extensively on professional ethics since the 1990s, and has been involved in the Code's revisions and in the development of its supplements for program administrators and adult educators. She is co-author of *Ethics and the Early Childhood Educator* and co-author of the Focus on Ethics column that is a regular feature of NAEYC's journal, *Young Children*. She is also the lead author of *Planning and Administering Early Childhood Programs* (now in its 11th edition).

Eva Moravcik, MEd, is professor of early childhood education at Honolulu Community College, where she teaches undergraduate courses in early childhood education and is the site coordinator of the Leeward Community College Children's Center. She received her bachelor's and master's degrees at the University of Hawaii.

Professor Moravcik has been involved in early childhood teaching and advocacy in Hawaii for many years. She has served as president of the Hawaii AEYC and on the editorial board of NAEYC. She contributed to the Code's supplements for program administrators and adult educators and has participated in revisions of the Code.

Professor Moravcik is co-author of *Who Am I in the Lives of Children?* (now in its 10th edition), *Meaningful Curriculum for Young Children,* and the social studies curriculum *Discovering Me and My World*. She is a frequent presenter on topics related to early childhood, including ethics, curriculum, administration, assessment, and documentation.

Acknowledgments

We are thankful to many people who have over the years supported and inspired our work on professional ethics in early childhood education. First, we are honored to have been able to build on work on ethics begun by Lilian Katz and Evangeline Ward in the I970s. We thank Barbara Bowman, who initiated work on a code of ethics as president of NAEYC in I980, and Marilyn Smith, past executive director of NAEYC, for her support and encouragement of early efforts to develop the code. We continue to appreciate the tremendous contributions that Kenneth Kipnis, professor of philosophy at the University of Hawaii, has made to our understanding of professional ethics and to NAEYC's work on developing the Code and its supplements. We thank him for his ongoing interest, support, and guidance.

Many individuals have contributed to the development and refinement of this manuscript. Thanks to Ingrid Anderson, Portland State University, for her careful reading of Chapter 2 and her insightful comments and suggestions; to Robyn Chun, University of Hawaii, for helping to develop materials and strategies for teaching ethical analysis to graduate students; to Sherry Nolte, who read and gave us valuable feedback on a draft of this book and allowed us to adapt activities from the program manual of the PACE (Professional and Career Education for Early Childhood) Program at Honolulu Community College; and to Cheryl Foster and Doris Christensen for sharing activities that they developed for teaching ethics. We are also appreciative of Cynthia Paris's insights and wise counsel, and thank Isabel Baker, president of The Book Vine for Children, for her suggestions for children's books that illustrate issues of morality and ethics.

We were fortunate to be able to draw on resources related to teaching early childhood professional ethics developed in Australia and Canada. We were inspired to write this book by *Getting Ethical: A Resource Book for Workshop Leaders*, written by Lyn Fasoli and Chris Woodrow for the Australian Early Childhood Association. We continue to be indebted to what we learned from it.

Thank you to Peter Pizzolongo, NAEYC's former associate executive director, Professional Development Solutions, for his ongoing interest, support, and participation in work on ethics, and to Kathy Charner, NAEYC's editor-in-chief, Books and Related Resources, for guiding us in the process of writing this second edition.

Most important, we acknowledge the contributions of our students, as well as the teachers, program administrators, teacher educators, and other interested professionals who have participated in our classes and attended our training sessions. Their interest in professional ethics and their commitment to young children and their families have encouraged us to write about teaching the Code. And we are grateful to all the early childhood educators who have told us stories about the ethical challenges they encountered in their work with children and families. Their stories have helped to make ethics come alive.

Thanks for purchasing

Teaching the NAEYC Code of Ethical Conduct: A Resource Guide

You may also be interested in the following NAEYC resources:

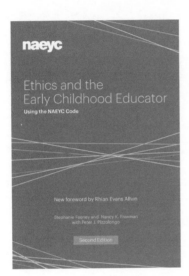

Ethics and the Early Childhood Educator: Using the NAEYC Code (2nd ed.)

By Stephanie Feeney & Nancy K. Freeman, With Peter J. Pizzolongo

Bestseller! *Ethics and the Early Childhood Educator* seeks to inform and guide those who work with children and families through the tough decisions they encounter. In this second edition, the authors provide new examples and questions intended to stimulate reflection and discussion on critical issues facing early childhood educators. (With a new cover and new foreword written by Rhian Evans Allvin)

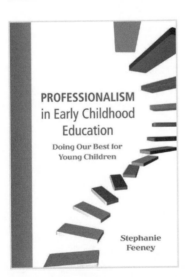

Professionalism in Early Childhood Education: Doing Our Best for Young Children

By Stephanie Feeney

Written for those entering the field or striving to grow within the profession, this book helps readers understand the nature of the profession, what it means to behave in a professional way, and where they stand in their own professional journey.